• Dog Breed Handbooks •

Dachshund

• DOG BREED HANDBOOKS •
DACHSHUND

BRUCE FOGLE, DVM

SPECIAL PHOTOGRAPHY BY
TRACY MORGAN

www.dk.com

A DK PUBLISHING BOOK
www.dk.com

Project Editor NIC KYNASTON
Art Editor STEFAN MORRIS
Editor KAREN O'BRIEN
Designer CLARE DRISCOLL
Managing Editor FRANCIS RITTER
Managing Art Editor DEREK COOMBES
DTP Designer SONIA CHARBONNIER
Picture Researcher MELISSA ALBANY
Production Controller RUTH CHARLTON
US Editor LAAREN BROWN

First American Edition 1997
First published as a Dorling Kindersley paperback 1999
4 6 8 10 9 7 5 3

Published in the United States by DK Publishing Inc.,
95 Madison Avenue, New York, New York 10016

First published in Great Britain in 1997
by Dorling Kindersley Limited,
9 Henrietta St, London WC2E 8PS

Library of Congress Cataloging-in-Publication Data

Fogle, Bruce
    Dachshund / by Bruce Fogle. – 1st American ed.
    p.   cm – (Dog breed handbooks)
    Includes index.
    ISBN 0-7894-1613-1
    ISBN 0-7894-4193-4 pbf
    1. Dachshunds. I. Title. II. Series: Fogle, Bruce.
Dog breed handbooks
SF 429.D25F64   1997   96–46078
636.7'53–dc20   CIP

Reproduced by Colourscan, Singapore
Printed in Hong Kong by Wing King Tong

CONTENTS

INTRODUCTION

It seems difficult to believe that the lovable Dachshund is a distant relative of the wolf

WE LIKE TO THINK that humans domesticated the dog, but this is only partly true. Although the dog has been our companion for longer than any other species of animal, we did not actively domesticate it. About 12,000 years ago, our ancestors in Asia founded permanent settlements. Local Asiatic wolves – sociable by nature – were attracted to these locations and moved into surrounding areas to scavenge for food. Since natural food was scarce, only the smallest and least fearful of the wolves survived their new environment. People recognized the potential value of orphan "wolf-dog" puppies raised within these communities as guard dogs and later as hunting companions.

The first evidence of dwarfing in the selective breeding of dogs can be traced back to ancient Egypt

ADAPTATION OF THE BREEDS

By about 6,000 years ago, selective breeding by humans had already produced dogs with virtually all of the characteristics that exist today, including miniaturization. The first evidence of dwarfing, the shortening of long bones, appeared about 3,000 years ago in Egypt, although it is unlikely that those short-legged dogs are related to today's Dachshund. In Europe, short-legged dogs can be traced back to the 16th century, when they were first bred to accompany hunters on foot, creating the ancestor of the modern Dachshund breed.

European hunters used short-legged hounds to run foxes, badgers, and rabbits to ground where the terrain prevented hunting on horseback

The Dachshund's small size and affectionate nature have made it a traditional favorite with children

THE EARTH DOG

By the 18th century, hunters, by selective breeding, had shortened the long bones in hounds and produced the Dachshund, a dog that could go to the ground after game such as badgers. These dwarfed hounds, which had shortened limbs but standard-sized bodies, were easier for the hunters to keep up with and could enter holes to confront prey. German foresters and gamekeepers subsequently reduced the body size of the Dachshund to create today's Miniature, which is small enough to give chase down a rabbit hole.

Although bred to be aggressive in the hunt, Dachshunds make loyal, gentle companions

THE IDEAL COMPANION

When raised as a member of the family, the Dachshund is an affable companion but also a robustly physical house-dog, willing to raise the alarm at the sight or sound of intruders. Working Dachshunds have particularly sturdy legs and chests that are well clear of the ground, while Dachshunds bred for show sometimes have shorter legs and a slighter build. Dachshunds make practical and delightful pets in urban environments, where daily exercise tends to be limited to local parks; the dog's short legs mean that it can be adequately exercised in a relatively small space.

Characteristically, the Dachshund is most often compared with the hound and the terrier

THE IDEAL CHOICE

FEW BREEDS OF DOG could be said to combine the vitality and distinctive personality of the Dachshund in one neat, sausage-like package. Its three coat types and wide range of colors add to the dog's popularity, while Miniature types make particularly ideal pets for city dwellers with limited space.

PART OF THE FAMILY

Remember that your cute Dachshund puppy will grow into a well-sized adult dog, especially if it is a Standard, and will need looking after for up to 14 years. Like a child, it depends on you to provide its nutrition, education, and well-being. Consider the amount of time you can dedicate to your dog, the space available in your home, the cost of veterinary attention, and the seasonal molting of long or wire hair. Do not forget to allow for your pet's food requirements too, since the Dachshund is one of the dog world's most prolific eaters!

PORTABLE FRIEND

The tiny Miniature Dachshund is perfectly suited for urban apartment dwellers who have limited space or for those who simply prefer to carry their dogs from home to the area where their dog can exercise and play. The Miniature's diminutive size also makes it an ideal companion if you are physically unable to provide vigorous exercise or long walks for your pet.

INDEPENDENT SPIRITS

Dachshunds generally have a confident, hearty nature, so early experience and good training is vital for molding them into affable, rewarding companions. You must be willing to invest time introducing your dog to new settings and training it to behave responsibly when it encounters unfamiliar situations.

Dog must be taught to behave well

A NATURALLY ACTIVE BREED

Nowadays a popular household pet, the Dachshund was originally bred as an active hunting dog, small enough to follow game into undergrowth and holes. Today, the Dachshund is still Germany's most effective earth dog and is used in a working role.

Despite its size, the Dachshund is not a lap-dog and, like most breeds, needs vigorous outdoor exercise. Your Dachshund will love to delve into rough terrain and water, so be prepared for a muddy, matted coat, especially if you have the long-haired type.

WHICH COAT TYPE?

There are striking visual differences between smooth-, wire-, and long-haired Dachshunds. The coats of smooth-haired dogs require less maintenance than those of most other breeds. Be sure to research how much grooming each coat type demands before you make your choice.

A LOYAL PROTECTOR

Although most dogs are kept as companions, even the smallest also provides security through its vigilance and superior senses. Due to its innate temperament, even the Miniature Dachshund is a natural guardian, willing to defend its home and to warn when visitors are approaching. All Dachshunds tend to be vigorously alert and are very vocal protectors. However, they must be trained to do so in a socially acceptable manner. Early introduction to other animals and to unfamiliar people is important.

SMOOTH-HAIRED DACHSHUND

THE MOST WELL KNOWN and probably the oldest type of Dachshund is the smooth-haired variety, with long- and wire-haired types selectively bred later from short-haired stock. The smooth-haired Dachshund's coat is as soft as velvet to the touch, and the breed's lively, inquisitive character makes it both a rewarding pet and a useful working dog.

BRIGHT AND DEVOTED COMPANION

The alert, quizzical look of this black-and-tan Standard-sized male epitomizes the lively spirit of the Dachshund. The dogs also make endearingly loyal pets, often displaying single-minded devotion to their owners. While smooth-, long-, and wire-haired dogs may look different, in practice there are only slight variations in temperament and behavior among Dachshunds of different coat types and colors.

SKIN
Supple, yet snugly fitting all parts of body, with virtually no wrinkles, puckers, or folds

COAT
Dense, short, shiny, and smooth; evenly distributed with no thin patches

TAIL
Continues line of spine in subtle curve; hair on underside of tail coarse in texture

LONG, LEAN, AND MUSCULAR

With its close-fitting skin and sleek coat, the smooth-haired Dachshund displays the breed's powerful, well-muscled physique to fine advantage. Although the legs are short in comparison with the length of the body, movement is surprisingly fluid and easy. The Dachshund's strong forequarters, combined with its low build, make it the ideal working dog for "going to ground" in search of game.

EYES
Prominent bridge between medium-sized eyes

NOSE
Black and well rounded, not cornered or sharp

DACHSHUND SIZES

There are several different sizes of Dachshund. In Britain and the United States, there are two official categories – the Standard and the Miniature – while in some other countries an additional, intermediate, size classification has been defined, sometimes called the Medium. Size is also measured differently from country to country; in Britain and the United States, the weight of the dog determines its category, while in many other nations the Dachshund is classified according to its chest circumference.

SKULL
Slightly arched, gradually sloping into muzzle

JAW
Wide-opening jaw bones; lips well stretched, neatly covering lower jaw

A VERSATILE, WORLD-CLASS DOG

The Dachshund is among Germany's most famous exports. In many parts of northern Europe, it is not uncommon to see Dachshunds in an active working role. Their keen sense of smell and unique shape suit them for a variety of hunting and tracking tasks.

TEETH
Strongly developed, with powerful canines; upper teeth closely overlap lower in perfect "scissors" bite

BACK
Level and full muscled, lying in straight line between shoulders and loin

NECK
Reasonably long and muscular, set at angle of 50–60° to length of body

CHEST
Deep and full, with sturdy rib cage and prominent, oval-shaped breastbone

LEGS
Shortened long bones with large joints

STANDARD DACHSHUND MEASUREMENTS (AMERICAN BREED STANDARD)

Ideal weight:
16–32 lb (7–14 kg)
There is no separate weight stipulated for males or females

6 ft
(1.8m)

LONG-HAIRED DACHSHUND

A LONG, SILKY COAT, gentle looks, and dignity of carriage are the most defining characteristics of the long-haired Dachshund. The exact origins of this attractive variety are unclear, but it appears to have existed for nearly as long as the smooth-haired type. Like all Dachshunds, its personality is engagingly affectionate and outgoing.

HEAD
Narrow skull, refined and well proportioned

PROUD BEARING
Known for its erect, proud carriage and dignified appearance, the long-haired Dachshund is often described as aristocratic in looks. However, it is also heavy boned, strong, and compact, revealing its original working role as a hunting dog.

EARS
Long-hanging, covered with silky, luxurious hair, and set just above eyes

HINDQUARTERS
Sound and broad, not angled too high; feathering silky, not fluffy

GENEALOGY

The ancestry of the long-haired Dachshund remains unconfirmed. One major theory is that this variety was produced some 200 years ago by cross-breeding the smooth-haired Dachshund with a small Spaniel, and then miniaturizing the result. However, other genealogists have traced the early development of the long-haired Dachshund back to 16th-century Germany, when the Badger Digger was crossed with the now-extinct German Gun Dog. Whatever its exact history, over the generations this variety's profuse, wavy coat has gradually become neater and lighter.

TAIL
Long at base and tapering to tip, with feathering abundant enough to hang as flag

THE LONG-HAIRED COAT

The coat should be long and silky, lying close to the body, without any tendency to rise or curl. Its appearance should be glossy. Feathering should not be too profuse, since this may hinder the dog's working ability. Hair should be shortest on the back and longest on the

EYES
*Usually
dark brown,
adding to
gentle look
of face*

MUZZLE
*Tapers into small,
fine nose; length of
muzzle slightly
exceeds that of skull*

EXTRA LENGTH OF BODY
Length of body is particularly vital in the
long-haired Dachshund. Since a long coat
can somewhat obscure physical contours, an
exaggerated length is required to retain the
breed's correct symmetry. A full coat will not
hide anatomical faults from a good judge.

BACK
*Top line of body is
long, strong, and level,
with slight arch above
loin; shoulders even*

EARS
*Positioned not
too far forward;
hair on outside
of ears well
feathered*

NECK
*Long and finely
arched to carry
head elegantly;
hair under neck
long and frilled*

FOREQUARTERS
*Wide shoulder blades
and solid chest; strong
upper legs with hard,
supple muscles*

underside and tail. The ideal coat grows
slowly; puppies that are full-coated at 10
or 12 months rarely carry perfect coats as
adults. Coat loss at molting time varies
between individual long-haired Dachshunds.

MEDIUM DACHSHUND MEASUREMENTS
(EUROPEAN BREED STANDARD)

Chest circumference (15 months and older):
14 in (35 cm) (maximum)
Ideal weight:
FEMALE up to 14 lbs (6.5 kg)
MALE up to 15 lbs (7 kg)
This category not recognized worldwide

6 ft
(1.8 m)

WIRE-HAIRED DACHSHUND

THE WIRE-HAIRED VARIETY is the most terrierlike of all Dachshunds, with a coarse top coat, a dense undercoat, and a face framed by distinctive whiskers. Developed primarily through breeding smooth-haired Dachshunds with rough-haired Pinschers and Dandie Dinmont Terriers, they make excellent working dogs and lively, extroverted pets.

ALERT AND READY FOR ACTION

Standing firmly on a compact, well-muscled frame with the head held confidently aloft, the wire-haired Dachshund's lively, thoughtful expression reflects its spirited and gregarious character and boundless energy for work and play. Its distinctive whiskers and beard give it a wise, serious expression that belies its sense of adventure. There is little variation in temperament between Standard, Medium, and Miniature wire-haired dogs.

EYES
Almond-shaped, set obliquely

HEAD
Long, tapering uniformly to tip of nose with moderate indentation; skull shallowly domed

COAT
Short, straight, harsh top coat with dense undercoat; bearded chin and bushy eyebrows, while hair on legs is quite smooth

MUZZLE
Strong jaw, neither too square nor pointed; immense biting and holding strength

FOREQUARTERS
Robust, well-ribbed chest and powerful front legs, short but strongly boned

FEET
Full at front, hind paws smaller and narrower; neatly furnished with harsh coat

TORSO
Sufficiently clear of ground to allow free movement

EARS
Well rounded, not folded or pointed; hair almost smooth

SKULL
Prominent ridges over eyes, making skull seem broad

DEVELOPMENT OF A TYPE

Although harsh-coated Dachshunds are recorded as far back as the late 18th century, the wire-haired Dachshund is the most recent type to have been developed by breeders. Terrier and Pinscher stock have given it verve and courage, as well as a unique appearance. Mating with Miniature breeds created a dog that could pursue small, burrowing prey.

GOOD-NATURED VIVACIOUS BREED

The amiable, expressive look of this wire-haired female exemplifies the breed's loyal and engaging temperament, and reflects an alert, responsive, and affectionate nature.

STRONG IN BODY AND CHARACTER

The Dachshund's long, low-slung physique, fine nose, and powerfully built forequarters make it an ideal "going to ground" tracker. As natural hunters, Dachshunds can at times exhibit a bravery that verges on rashness.

BACK
Long, muscular body features level back with sloping shoulders

TAIL
Slightly curved, but without kinks or twists, not carried too high or touching ground at rest

UNDERCOAT
Fine hair forms protective layer under coarser top coat

MINIATURE DACHSHUND MEASUREMENTS (AMERICAN BREED STANDARD)

Ideal weight:
11lb (5 kg) and under
There is no separate weight stipulated for males or females; dogs compete at this weight at 12 months and older

6 ft
(1.8 m)

BEHAVIOR PROFILE

EVERY DOG'S PERSONALITY is shaped in part by its early experiences within the litter and later with you. Heredity is equally important, which is why, regardless of upbringing, each breed has its own behavior profile. The Dachshund's lively nature and loyalty make it a popular companion.

TRAINABILITY/OBEDIENCE

Dachshunds are intelligent dogs and can be trained quickly if you start early. Although sometimes known to be stubborn, they are easier to train than Shih Tzus or West Highland White Terriers, but more difficult than Miniature Poodles or Cocker Spaniels.

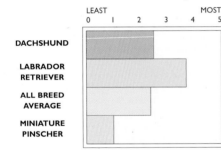

PLAYFULNESS WITH OTHER DOGS

Never bred to work in packs, Dachshunds are consequently slightly less playful with other dogs than average – about the same as Rottweilers and Yorkshire Terriers. However, early socialization with other dogs can increase playfulness in later life.

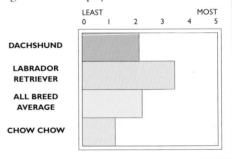

BARKING TO PROTECT THE HOME

There are few breeds that are as efficient as Dachshunds at barking to protect the home. Only Australian Cattle Dogs, German Shepherds, Fox Terriers, Toy Poodles, and Lhasa Apsos are as vocal. Nuisance barking can be controlled through early training.

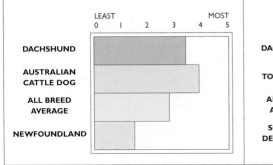

EXCITABILITY

Dachshunds are only slightly more excitable than the average breed, about the same as Beagles, Shih Tzus, and Australian Kelpies. Excitability has a strong genetic basis; if the mother is excitable, there is a strong chance that your puppy has inherited that trait.

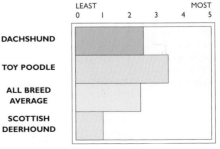

How to Use the Behavior Charts

In a recent study, vets and dog breeders assessed over 100 breeds, rating each on a scale of 0–5 for specific personality traits, with 0 representing the lowest score among all dogs and 5 the highest. Here, for eight different behaviors, the Dachshund is compared with the statistically "average" canine, as well as with breeds rated at both extremes for each characteristic. The findings in the charts below do not take the dog's sex or breed variants into consideration.

Reliable with Strange Children

Dachshunds, especially Miniature smooth-haireds, are likely to view strange children with suspicion, especially in their own homes. Corgis, Miniature Pinschers, and Fox Terriers share this trait. Monitor meetings between your Dachshund and new children.

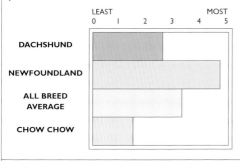

LEAST 0 1 2 3 4 5 MOST

- DACHSHUND
- NEWFOUNDLAND
- ALL BREED AVERAGE
- CHOW CHOW

Calm in New Circumstances

Traditionally, there has never been pressure to breed the Dachshund selectively for calmness. In fact, this dog has been bred to be vigorously alert in new situations. Like the Cocker Spaniel, the Dachshund is always responsive and ready for activity.

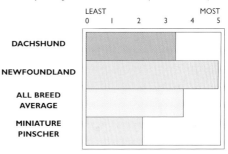

LEAST 0 1 2 3 4 5 MOST

- DACHSHUND
- NEWFOUNDLAND
- ALL BREED AVERAGE
- MINIATURE PINSCHER

Destructive when Alone

When left unattended at home, Dachshunds are more likely to damage furnishings than other, less excitable, breeds. In this regard, they are similar to Boxers and Miniature Schnauzers. Provide your dog with mental stimulation to reduce destructive tendencies.

LEAST 0 1 2 3 4 5 MOST

- DACHSHUND
- DOBERMAN
- ALL BREED AVERAGE
- NEWFOUNDLAND

House Trainable

Virtually all dogs respond well to house training, and while Dachshunds are slightly poorer than average, they are comparable to Bassett Hounds, Beagles, and Lhasa Apsos. This characteristic is influenced more by early training patterns than by breeding.

LEAST 0 1 2 3 4 5 MOST

- DACHSHUND
- LABRADOR/ GERMAN SHEPHERD
- ALL BREED AVERAGE
- YORKSHIRE TERRIER/ TOY POODLE

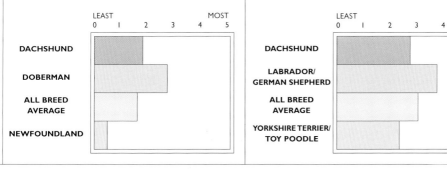

COATS AND COLORS

DACHSHUNDS APPEAR IN A WIDE range of solid and mixed colors —
from rich one-color coats, such as chocolate and various
shades of red, to classic two-toned black-and-tans. Brindle
is an even mixture of black hair with a lighter color,
while a dapple coat has an elegant, mottled pattern.

HISTORY OF COAT COLORS

When Dachshunds' coat colors were first
recorded in 1701, they were described as
ranging from "gray to black." By 1848,
this had changed to "yellow, or black
with yellow extremities." Cross-breeding
with Bavarian Mountain Hound and
French Pyrenean Pointer stock then
introduced various shades of red. All
colors seen today — including reds,
shaded reds, chocolates, black-and-tans,
brindles, and dapples — are genetic
variations that stem from this stock.

*Pale red pigment
makes dog's coat
appear brown
with cream flecks*

LIGHT CHOCOLATE
This long-haired Dachshund has
an attractive and unusual light
chocolate color, the
result of cross-
breeding a red
coat with a
chocolate.

SHADES OF RED
These three dogs show
the range in shade of
red coats. On the
far left is a pure
red or golden,
the middle dog is
a shaded red with
a small amount of
black in its coat,
and on the right
is a red brindle.

DAPPLES AND BRINDLES

LONG-HAIRED BRINDLE
This long-haired female is a chocolate brindle. All brindles have an even mixture of black hairs with hairs of a lighter color throughout their coat. Brindle coats most often occur in long- and wire-haired dogs; smooth-haired brindle Dachshunds are rarely seen.

WIRE-HAIRED BRINDLE
The coat of this male wire-haired brindle is a vibrant mixture of black and red hairs. On wire-haired dogs, the hair on the face is often grown longer to produce the distinctive "whiskers" that give the dog its distinguished appearance. Wire-haired dogs should have their coats stripped of excess hair about once every three months.

LONG-HAIRED SILVER DAPPLE
The first record of the dapple can be traced back to 1797, making it one of the oldest Dachshund coat patterns. Dapples have a unique appearance, and can be silver, chocolate, or red. This silver male has a silver-gray base coat with an even mixture of white and black hairs, giving a roan, or varied, effect overall.

COAT COLOR GENEALOGY

A puppy's coat color is determined by the genes that it inherits from its parents. Some colors are dominant over others; for example, if a pure-bred red dog is mated with a black-and-tan, all puppies will be red, though they will carry the black-and-tan gene. Thus, some future offspring of these red puppies could be black-and-tan dogs. Red is also dominant over chocolate, as is black-and-tan. The brindle coat pattern is dominant over black-and-tan, red, and chocolate.

LOOKS AND PERSONALITY

A DACHSHUND'S CHARACTER can be influenced by its size and coat type. Vets and breeders report that there are some significant differences in temperament between the various sizes, and that smooth-, long-, and wire-haired Dachshunds tend to display certain specific behavioral traits.

SIZE AND TEMPERAMENT

Dachshunds were first miniaturized in the mid-18th century when they were bred by hunters to pursue small game into their holes. Continued selective breeding produced the Miniature Dachshund, a dog practically suited to urban environments because of its size. However, vets and breeders report that larger Dachshunds are frequently less nervous than Miniatures; most Standards do not behave as aggressively when provoked, and they usually respond more effectively to training.

COAT TYPE AND CHARACTER

Although smooth-, long-, and wire-haired Dachshunds all come from the same basic genetic stock, they can manifest discernably different character traits. Wire-haired dogs are often the most willing to respond to obedience training, while long-haired Dachshunds seem to be the most aloof and independent. Smooth-haired dogs are reported to be the

most territorial of the breed, and the most likely to bark at intruders. It is said that owners' personalities rub off on their dogs and that an easy-going, placid person will tend to produce a Dachshund with similar characteristics. Most breeders and vets agree that nurture is as important as nature. A dog given firm but fair obedience training early in life, along with a healthy environment and plenty of exercise, is likely to be well adjusted, outgoing, and contented.

Coat-Related Differences

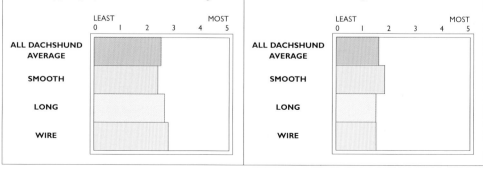

In a survey assessing over 100 breeds of dog, vets and breeders answered questions about Dachshunds' behavior patterns according to coat type. The lowest possible score shown on the charts is 0, and the highest is 5. Note that these results apply to the breed as a whole, not to individual dogs. In practice, experienced dog handlers recommend that the best way to assess the mature temperament of a young dog is to observe the disposition of its parents.

Nervous in New Situations

In general, long- and wire-haired Dachshunds are significantly calmer than smooth-haired types, usually displaying less fear and behaving less aggressively in strange environments or circumstances. This characteristic, however, depends strongly on individual heredity.

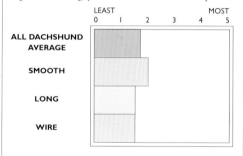

Reliable with Strange Children

Smooth-haired Dachshunds tend to be less reliable than long- and wire-haired ones in situations such as being confronted with an unknown five-year-old child on their own territory. They also accept adult strangers less willingly than dogs of other coat types.

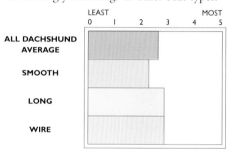

Needs Physical Activity

Although all Dachshunds are generally energetic, responsive, and receptive to play, long- and wire-haired dogs seem to demand slightly more physical exercise than smooth-haireds. There is little difference, however, in each type's playfulness with other dogs.

LEAST 0 1 2 3 4 5 MOST

ALL DACHSHUND AVERAGE
SMOOTH
LONG
WIRE

Disobedient toward Owner

Dachshunds' celebrated independence of spirit can at times translate into disobedience toward their owners. While each type is equally trainable, smooth-haired dogs are considered somewhat more likely to disobey their owners than long- and wire-haireds.

LEAST 0 1 2 3 4 5 MOST

ALL DACHSHUND AVERAGE
SMOOTH
LONG
WIRE

SEX AND TYPE DIFFERENCES

MALE AND FEMALE DACHSHUNDS often exhibit some basic differences in behavior. Breeding also produces specific physical variations between Dachshunds intended for show and those reared as working dogs. The greatest difference between pet and show Dachshunds is in their early training.

PHYSIQUE AND TEMPERAMENT: THE SEXES COMPARED

Male Dachshunds are only marginally larger than females, and they share similarly vibrant, spirited characters. There is little difference between the sexes in trainability, nervousness, eagerness to play with other dogs, barking for attention, or enjoyment at being petted.

Expression reflects desire to please

Body is somewhat slighter than male's

ALERT, AMIABLE FEMALE

Female Dachshunds are generally affable and responsive, yet retain an independent nature. Smooth-haired females may be slightly more nervous and disobedient than males, while female long-haireds are considered moderately more excitable. Female Dachshunds of all types are thought to need just a little less physical activity than males.

CONFIDENT, ACTIVE MALE

Males can be more assertive than females, and are more likely to bark to protect their homes. They are also more wary of strangers when on their own territory. However, unlike some breeds, male Dachshunds are no more inclined than females to dominate unfamiliar dogs, or to resent being handled or disciplined.

GENDER-SPECIFIC MEDICAL PROBLEMS

A variety of diseases are caused or influenced by sex hormones. Unless spayed early in life, females of all breeds may suffer from breast cancer or pyometra, a womb infection. Uncastrated males sometimes develop perianal tumors, testicular cancer, or prostate inflammation, with associated pain or bleeding during urination. Neutering is part of the preferred treatment for all gender-related medical conditions. With Dachshunds in particular, the diet should be carefully controlled to prevent weight gain after neutering.

SHOW OR WORKING TYPE?

SHOW DOGS

The majority of Dachshunds are specifically bred to conform to formal show standards, which call for a deep chest and short legs. Having been selected for beauty, show dogs are then trained from an early age in show-ring deportment. Proper carriage, a graceful, flowing gait, and calm acceptance of inspection from the judges are all vital to a winning show performance.

Prize-winning Dachshund carries head and neck in elegant, dignified manner

Hindquarters are placed so that legs assume correct show stance

Short legs and full chest meet official standards of breed

Weatherproof wire-haired coat protects working dog in undergrowth and water

Miniature type ideally suited for "going to ground" in hunt

Relatively long, muscular legs raise chest well clear of ground for easy movement

WORKING DACHSHUNDS

The Dachshund has not lost its hunting instinct, although today it rarely has the opportunity to work. However, in some parts of Europe, particularly in Germany, Dachshunds are still bred primarily for this role. Working dogs are selected for their small size and ability to negotiate narrow burrows. This requires a higher, shallower chest and longer, more powerful front legs than a typical Dachshund. Working dogs are often leaner in build than show dogs because their activities enhance body tone.

EFFECTS OF NEUTERING

Dogs may be neutered not only as a means of population control, but also to help treat behavioral problems; however, this is less common in Dachshunds than in some other breeds. In males, neutering reduces aggression toward other dogs, but not toward people. Neutering has little impact on female personality, except in very dominant bitches, whose willfulness may actually be enhanced.

THE RIGHT START

BEFORE MAKING THE DECISION to acquire a Dachshund, think hard about how a dog would fit in with your lifestyle. Seek plenty of advice so that you can make a responsible choice. Your local vet or dog training club are good sources of information. If buying a dog, check that the price includes a full veterinary examination.

WHERE TO BUY AND WHAT TO LOOK FOR

ANIMAL RESCUE CENTERS
Dog shelters and animal rescue leagues sometimes have adult Dachshunds in need of new homes. These dogs can make very devoted pets, but bear in mind that their past experiences may mean that they have unexpected behavioral problems.

CONSULTING EXPERTS
Vets and their staff are an excellent source of free, unbiased information on what to look for and where to find a healthy Dachshund. They are often aware of the breed's medical problems and any behavioral difficulties that could arise.

A PUPPY OR AN ADULT DOG?

No one would deny that Dachshund puppies are incredibly appealing, but they are also very lively, and will demand a lot of your time and attention in order to become house-trained and to learn obedience. Be certain that you can manage such a commitment, and try to visit several litters before making your final choice. Take note of the temperament of the mother and, if possible, the father, too; this will give you some idea of the character your dog may develop. If you decide that you want a trained adult dog, find out as much as you can in advance about its personality to ensure that it will be a suitable pet for you.

Healthy puppy feels firm and is surprisingly heavy

SETTLING IN AT HOME

Secure crate allows gentle exposure to new environment

ARRIVING HOME

Your puppy is likely to feel disoriented when it first arrives in your home. Try to make its new environment less daunting by confining it to one room and providing it with its own "den" – a crate where it can feel secure. Make the place inviting by placing food, water, and a chewable toy inside, and leave the door open. Lay down some soft bedding in one section of the crate and an equal area of newspaper for toileting.

GETTING ACQUAINTED

Your puppy's first night away from its mother in new surroundings is the hardest, but it should settle down eventually and sleep. If you prefer, you can take your puppy's crate into your bedroom so that you can keep an eye on it. After it has sufficiently rested, bring in any other pets you may have. Keep the puppy's crate door closed so that you can control their first meetings.

HEALTH CHECKS FOR YOUR NEW DOG

When buying a puppy, it is wise to have it examined by your vet to ensure that it is healthy, with no signs of infectious disease, malnutrition, or parasites. You should make your purchase of the dog provisional upon its being given a clean bill of health. Breeders should also supply you with documents verifying that the puppy's parents are free from a variety of hereditary disorders. The law states that if a puppy is not healthy at the time of sale, then you are entitled to a refund or replacement.

MEET THE PARENTS

It is advisable, whenever possible, to buy your dog directly from a reputable breeder. Avoid puppy farms or mills, since they often keep dogs in inhumane conditions and pay little attention to the puppies' health. Some advertisements in newspapers are fronts for puppy farms – be suspicious if you visit a private address and are not allowed to see the litter's mother. Also be wary of some pet stores – they can be breeding grounds for a range of infectious diseases and may supply you with an unhealthy individual purchased from a puppy farm.

Early Training

DACHSHUNDS ARE ADEPT AT LEARNING and respond willingly when rewarded with praise, petting, food treats, or stimulating toys. Start gentle obedience and house training as soon as you bring your puppy home, and make regular contact with other dogs to ensure proper social development.

Learning with Rewards

Stroking Reward
Physical contact is a very powerful reward for your puppy. Your Dachshund will want to be stroked often, but do not comply on demand. Instead, give a gentle command, then reward obedience with petting.

Puppy knows it has done well when it hears "Good dog!"

Touching head can be seen as threat; stroke chest or side instead

Verbal Praise
Dachshunds are enthusiastic pupils. Even an eight-week-old puppy will understand when you are genuinely pleased with its behavior. Positive words of praise should always accompany food and touch rewards.

Acquiring Social Skills

A puppy's ability to learn is at its greatest very early in life, and only through ongoing contact with other canines can it learn how to behave with strange dogs as an adult. If you do not own another dog, ask your vet to recommend or even help you to organize weekly "puppy parties" where puppies of a similar age can meet and play under supervision. When walking your puppy, try to avoid aggressive-looking dogs; confrontation can be traumatic for your pet.

Food Treat
Although most Dachshunds respond well to food rewards, some may be indifferent. Try a variety of snacks to discover which your puppy likes best, then use these as rewards, combined with plenty of verbal praise.

Treat reinforces good behavior

TOYS FOR YOUR NEW PUPPY

Put toys away to show that they belong to you

Dog learns that owner controls play

TOYS FOR CHEWING AND PLAYING

As natural hunters, Dachshunds enjoy playing with toys, especially squeaky ones. Choose no more than four toys that are fun to chase, retrieve, capture, and chew. After play, let your puppy see you put the toys away; this helps to discourage possessiveness, more common in Dachshunds than in some other breeds.

TOYS AS REWARD AND COMFORT

Toys left lying around soon become boring, while those brought out on special occasions are transformed into exciting rewards. Used selectively, toys can serve as effective training aids. When you leave your dog alone, provide it with a toy for comforting distraction.

Rope chew toy occupies puppy and exercises jaw muscles

HOUSE TRAINING INDOORS AND OUT

Praise puppy when it eliminates on newspaper

MOVING OUTSIDE

Start outdoor training as soon as possible. A three-month-old Dachshund needs to empty its bladder once every three hours. Take a small piece of soiled paper with you; the puppy will smell its own scent and be encouraged to transfer toileting outside. As it eliminates, say "Hurry up"; this will train your dog to relieve itself on that command.

PAPER TRAINING

Your puppy will usually need to eliminate after waking, eating, drinking, or exercise. It may signal this by putting its nose to the ground and sniffing. Quickly place the dog in an area covered with newspaper, then praise it when it eliminates. It is pointless to punish your puppy after an accident. If you catch it in the act in the wrong place, sternly say "No!" and take it to the paper or outside.

INTRODUCING OUTDOORS

YOUR PUPPY SHOULD EXPERIENCE the outside world as soon as possible. Check that your Dachshund has had all the vaccinations it needs for going out, and equip it with identification. Meet friends and their well-trained dogs to accustom your puppy to new situations in a controlled way.

IDENTIFICATION

STANDARD NAME TAG
Engraved or canister tags carry vital information, including your address and telephone number and, if possible, your veterinarian's emergency number. A dab of nail polish will prevent canisters from unscrewing.

PERMANENT METHODS
Inserted under the skin on the neck, a tiny transponder encased in glass can hold important data about your dog that can be "read" using a hand-held scanner. Painless tattoos, usually on the inside of the ear flap, are another means of recording registration details.

INTRODUCTION TO COLLAR AND LEASH

1 Training with a collar and leash can begin as soon as you take your puppy home. Start by letting the dog see and smell the collar. Then, avoiding eye contact, kneel beside your puppy and distract it with words while you put on the collar. Reward with food, physical contact, and praise. Play enthusiastically with your puppy for a while, then take the collar off. Your dog will soon learn that the collar is associated with rewards and will happily wear it.

Gently fit light, comfortable collar

2 Once your puppy is content with wearing its collar, kneel in front of it and attach a leash. Keeping the leash slack, entice your dog to one side with a toy or food reward. As it moves toward the reward, apply light tension to the leash. Praise the puppy and allow it to have the toy or treat.

Owner distracts puppy with toy

ENCOUNTERING OTHER DOGS

Arrange for a friend who has a well-behaved, placid dog to meet you while you are out walking your puppy. Your friend should instruct his dog to sit while you and your puppy approach. Reward your Dachshund's calmness with a food treat and praise. If you do not know people with dogs, you will find that other dog walkers are usually more than willing to help with this form of training. By creating situations where your dog meets others in circumstances that you control, your Dachshund learns that there is no need to be fearful of other dogs. Regular interaction with other puppies of a similar age will also help your dog to develop desirable canine social skills.

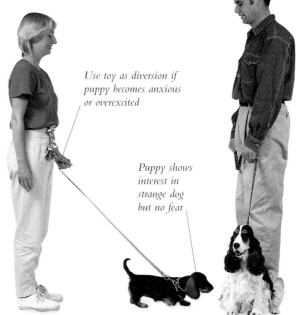

Use toy as diversion if puppy becomes anxious or overexcited

Puppy shows interest in strange dog but no fear

MEETING STRANGERS

Ask a friend to meet you and your dog outdoors. Your friend should kneel when greeting the puppy, to reduce the likelihood of its jumping up. Avoid eye contact with the dog since this can evoke an overly submissive response in a puppy.

Puppy will feel less threatened if it is greeted kneeling down

ESSENTIAL PUPPY INOCULATIONS

Your vet will vaccinate your puppy against diseases such as parvovirus, distemper, and hepatitis. He or she may advise that you avoid unfamiliar dogs for a few weeks. Regular contact with known healthy dogs should continue, however, to ensure proper social development.

FIRST ROUTINES

A PUPPY'S EARLY EXPERIENCES influence its adult personality, so you should establish rules early on. Train your Dachshund to be left alone, to come to you on command, and, most important, to understand that you and your family are its superiors and will not tolerate misbehavior.

ACCEPTING BEING LEFT ALONE

No matter how much you enjoy being with your new puppy, there will be times when you must leave it on its own. Train your young Dachshund to accept that this is part of its routine by leaving it in a room or in its crate with an interesting reward, such as a hollow toy containing a little peanut butter or cheese spread. Then quietly walk away, signaling "Wait." Gradually accustom your puppy to being left alone for longer periods.

Puppy is contented, left alone with toy

ASSERT YOUR LEADERSHIP

Some Dachshunds have a tendency to be pushy with their owners, to resist being groomed or handled, and even to snap at members of the household. Teach your dog the meaning of a stern "No!" If necessary, a painless, physical reprimand, such as mimicking its mother by grabbing the scruff of the neck, may be used very sparingly and just for theatrical effect.

Puppy knows it has done wrong and rolls over submissively

BRINGING UP MORE THAN ONE PUPPY

Puppies require a great deal of care and attention. If you do decide to bring up more than one puppy at a time, then try to train them individually. Although it requires organization, this method will achieve the most effective results in the shortest time. Even the most highly experienced dog handlers can find it difficult to maintain the concentration of several lively puppies all at the same time!

COMING TO YOU ON COMMAND

1 For safety and responsible control, your puppy must learn always to come to you on command. Use positive training by rewarding your puppy when it responds to a command. Put your dog's collar and leash on. Kneel close to the puppy, tucking the leash under your knees, and offer a reward.

Toy is used to encourage uninterested puppy

2 Call your puppy's name in a clear, friendly tone to attract its attention, and wave the reward in your outstretched hand. Do not apply tension to the leash; it is on to make sure that your puppy does not stray, not to reel it in. As your puppy starts to move, command it to come.

Owner uses the command "Come"

Make sure puppy does not strain at leash

3 Greet your puppy with open arms. Out of curiosity, it should start to walk toward you. As it moves forward, say "Good dog" in a friendly, enthusiastic voice. Never call your dog's name in order to discipline it – train it to understand that "Come" is always a positive command associated with praise or a reward. Carry out training sessions with your Dachshund just before mealtimes, when it should be at its most responsive and alert.

Puppy learns to walk toward owner when called

When puppy reaches you, reward with favorite toy

COME, SIT, DOWN, STAY

BASIC OBEDIENCE IS ESSENTIAL to your dog's safety and to harmonious relations with others. The Dachshund's independent spirit calls for patient training, started as early as possible. Use food treats or a squeaky toy to teach your puppy to come, sit, lie down, and stay, always keeping sessions short, positive, and fun.

COME AND SIT

Maintain eye contact with your puppy

1 Try to work in a quiet, narrow space such as a hallway, with no distractions. Holding the puppy on a loose leash, briskly and cheerfully call its name and let it see that you have a food treat in your hand. As it starts to move toward you, give the command "Come." If there is no reaction, you may need to bend down so that your puppy can clearly see the treat. Always be enthusiastic and encouraging, and while your puppy comes to you, praise it by saying "Good dog."

Leash is slack but can be gently pulled to reinforce command

Food treat held over puppy's head imposes sit position

Puppy watches intently, waiting for reward

2 When your puppy reaches you, move the treat above its head. To keep its eye on the food, the puppy will naturally sit. As it does so, issue the command "Sit" in a positive tone and immediately give the reward. Offer the treat calmly to avoid overexcitement. Repeat this exercise regularly, before each meal, when your puppy is hungry and receptive to food incentives. With practice, it should willingly respond to words alone.

THE UNRESPONSIVE PUPPY

Although most Dachshunds respond superbly to food rewards, try to plan training sessions for just before mealtimes when your puppy is hungriest. Begin in a quiet indoor environment before moving outside, where there are more distractions for a lively and curious dog. Train only for short periods when you, as well as your puppy, are mentally alert, and make certain that all commands are gently enforced. With a strong-willed puppy, use a leash to ensure that it complies. Keep lessons stimulating and fun, always finishing on a high note so that your puppy looks forward to the next session.

DOWN

Keep reward visible but held firmly until given

Grasp collar to assert control

STAY DOWN

Having positioned your puppy down, command "Stay." With the leash held loosely in your hand, and maintaining eye contact, get up and stand in front, repeating "Stay." Use a raised palm gesture rather than rewards; this will become a learned visual signal. In potentially hazardous situations, instant response to the "Stay" command is very important.

1 Seat your puppy and kneel beside it, securing the leash under one knee. Holding its collar with one hand, place a treat by its nose. If the puppy tries to get up, tuck its hindquarters under with your free hand and say "Sit." If it lunges for the food, use a less exciting squeaky toy.

2 Move the treat forward and down in an arc; your puppy will follow the food with its nose. As it starts to lie down, give the command "Down." If the puppy refuses, gently raise its front legs into a begging position, then lower it down, always rewarding compliance with hearty praise.

Do not over-praise puppy when giving food reward

3 Still holding the collar, continue to move the treat forward and down until your puppy is lying completely flat. Then reward the puppy with the treat and praise. Do not praise excessively, however, since this can excite your young Dachshund and be counterproductive.

Puppy stretches out to receive treat

TRAINING TO HEEL

AN OBEDIENT DACHSHUND who is heeling is an impressive sight. Make sure that walking your dog is a pleasure rather than a struggle by starting to heel at an early age. Begin training indoors before graduating outside, and postpone practice sessions until later if your puppy loses interest.

HEELING WITHOUT A LEASH

1 In a quiet indoor location, kneel to the right of your alert, seated puppy. Holding its collar in your left hand, speak your dog's name while showing it a food treat or another reward in your right hand.

2 Using the scent of the food to attract the puppy, get up and walk in a straight line while giving the command "Heel." Be ready to grasp the collar with your left hand and return your puppy to the correct heel position if it wanders. When you stop, give the command "Wait."

Puppy eagerly follows reward

3 Keeping the treat low to prevent your puppy from jumping up, bend your knees and turn right, drawing the food around as you move. Repeat the command "Heel." Your puppy will speed up to walk around you.

Train puppy to stay close to your leg

4 Teaching left turns is slightly more difficult. Hold the puppy's collar firmly with your left hand and give the command "Steady." Place the reward close to your puppy's mouth, then move it around to the left. Your Dachshund should follow the reward.

Heeling with a Leash

1 With the puppy to your left on a training leash, tell it to sit. Hold the lead and a food treat in your right hand, and the slack of the leash in your left. If your puppy lies down, return it to a sitting position by holding the treat to its nose.

Maintain eye contact as puppy waits for next command

Puppy sits obediently

2 Move forward with your left foot while giving the command "Heel." If your puppy pulls or collapses, return it to a sit with the treat. If it strays too far ahead, give the leash a light jerk to pull it back.

3 With the puppy beside you in the heel position; offer it the reward and say "Good dog." Repeat the "Sit. Heel. Wait." sequence. With each session, gradually increase the distance covered.

5 Once the right turn has been learned, begin left-turn training. Hold the treat in front of the puppy's nose to slow it down, while speeding up your own circling movement to the left. Keep the puppy close to your left leg and issue the command "Steady" as it follows you around.

4 After your puppy has learned to walk to heel in a straight line, teach it to turn to the right by guiding it with the treat. Do not pull or get angry; build up your dog's confidence with praise.

Puppy slows down while concentrating on food reward

INDOOR TRAINING

ALTHOUGH YOUR DACHSHUND loves being outdoors, it is likely to spend much of its time inside your home. Make sure that it understands basic house rules, and provide it with some space of its own. Give your dog plenty of attention and time, but always on your initiative, not on demand.

LEARNING TO WAIT PATIENTLY

Dogs were originally pack animals and followed a dominant pack leader. You should be this leader for your Dachshund – you are the boss who decides what happens and when. Some male Miniature Dachshunds have a tendency to demand constant attention if they think they will receive it; you should set the agenda. Make sure that you provide your Dachshund with its own personal space, which should include its bed or crate. It will learn to rest here when you are busy.

Bed is large enough for Dachshund to stretch out

SPENDING QUALITY TIME TOGETHER

Nurturing the bond between you and your dog is not only enjoyable for both of you but reinforces basic obedience training. It is also essential to your dog's well-being and development. Set aside time each day to play games with your Dachshund: these should provide a mixture of physical activity and mental stimulus. Be sure to vary the time of day and the type of play so that your dog will not expect a certain game at a particular time.

Playing together is fun, and keeps dog happy and alert

Meeting Visitors in the Home

Some Dachshunds, especially Miniatures, can be very territorial; make sure that your dog is not a nuisance by training it to sit when a guest arrives. This will reduce the likelihood of territory guarding – most common in male dogs – and help control the inclination that some Dachshunds have to go wild with over-excitement. Ask visitors to ignore your pet as they arrive; this will encourage it to remain calm. Reward your dog's good behavior with praise, a stroke, or a food treat.

Dog placidly accepts guest's presence

Relinquishing a Forbidden Item

Dachshunds, like many breeds of dog, have a desire to hoard household items such as dish towels, socks, and slippers, often keeping them in their bed. Reduce the potential for such possessive behavior by training your dog, using food treats, to drop and surrender any article willingly on command.

Use body language as well as words to convey your displeasure

Understanding What Is Wrong

Dogs will not know that they have done something wrong until this is made clear to them. For instance, lying on a comfortable chair seems perfectly natural to your Dachshund but may not be acceptable to you. Adopt an assertive stance and a stern tone of voice to reprimand your dog when it does something that is not permitted. Be suitably theatrical, and your dog will quickly learn your intentions. Good timing is essential; if you discipline your dog some time after the misbehavior, it will understand only that you are angry, but not what it has done wrong.

OUTSIDE THE HOME

FOR ITS OWN PROTECTION and the security of others, keep your Dachshund under safe control in your own garden and further afield. When planning a vacation, make sure that your dog will be comfortable if left with other people. Always provide a healthy, hazard-free environment for your pet.

HOME AND AWAY

If you need to put your dog in a kennel while you are away, visit recommended kennels and check them for cleanliness and security. An alternative is a dog-sitting service; your vet may be able to give you details of reliable agencies.

BE CONSIDERATE TO OTHERS

Always obey local dog-control regulations, and clean up after your dog outside. Carry a supply of plastic bags or a "poop scoop" and use special trash cans if available. Do not let your dog be a nuisance to others.

CONTROL OUTDOORS

HEAD HALTER
A fitted head halter offers more control than a collar, especially for willful Dachshunds. If your dog pulls on its leash, the momentum will pull its head downward and inhibit it.

HALF-CHOKE COLLAR
Fit the collar so that the soft webbing lies around your dog's throat, while the chain sits at the back of the neck. A tug on the leash will tighten the collar without causing pain.

MUZZLE
Apply a muzzle either to obey local laws or to prevent your dog from biting. Use a basket variety in the correct size and properly adjusted to permit panting and barking.

BODY HARNESS
A body harness is suitable for most Dachshunds. Make sure you select the right size for your dog. Pulling forward produces inhibiting tension on the whole body, not just on the neck as with a standard collar.

SAFE TRAVELING

Train your dog from an early age to travel contentedly with you by car. Miniature Dachshunds can be transported in a cat carrier securely belted in the back seat. Larger dogs can be strapped into the back seat with a special canine seat belt that, like a child's harness, attaches to the standard seat-belt anchors. Alternatively, restrict your dog to the rear of a station wagon behind a sturdy, custom-made dog grille, or secured in a good-sized wire cage.

CAR DANGERS

Heatstroke is among the most common causes of preventable death in dogs. Since a dog cannot sweat other than through its foot, excess body heat can be reduced only by panting. In hot conditions, the body temperature rises swiftly, sometimes within minutes, and if there is no escape, a dog can die. Never leave your dog in your car in warm or sunny weather – even when parked in the shade or with the window slightly opened. In cold weather, do not leave your dog in brilliant sunshine with the car engine running and the heater on high; this, too, can be lethal.

PLANNING A SAFE AND SECURE YARD

The greatest hazard presented by your yard is the risk of escape. Check that all fencing is sturdy, gate latches secure, and that hedges have no gaps. Install wire mesh where necessary. Keep all garden chemicals safely locked away, and if you have outdoor lighting, make sure that no cables are exposed and can be chewed. To prevent damage to your lawn, train your dog to use a specific site as its toilet. Store all trash and any gardening tools securely out of reach, and do not establish plants that may be poisonous to dogs. Always watch your dog carefully near a lit barbecue to ensure that it does not lick hot implements, and cover garden ponds to prevent your Dachshund from paddling.

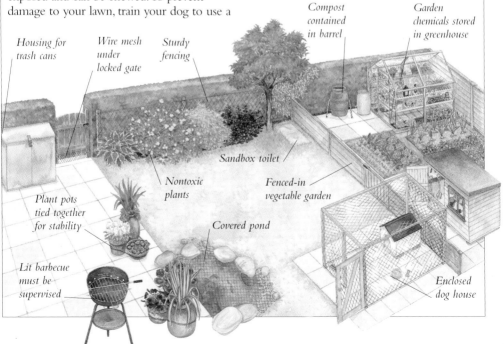

Housing for trash cans

Wire mesh under locked gate

Sturdy fencing

Compost contained in barrel

Garden chemicals stored in greenhouse

Sandbox toilet

Nontoxic plants

Fenced-in vegetable garden

Plant pots tied together for stability

Covered pond

Lit barbecue must be supervised

Enclosed dog house

CONSTRUCTIVE PLAY

DACHSHUNDS ARE ALERT AND LIVELY, and need mental stimulation as well as physical exercise. Create activities that utilize your pet's unique abilities; games that involve scent-trailing, retrieving, and carrying will be especially enjoyable for your dog. Use play to underscore obedience training and to have fun.

RETRIEVE ON COMMAND

Train your Dachshund to hold an object in its mouth and then to pick it up – use verbal praise for reward and encouragement. Progress to teaching the command "Fetch." Once your dog understands this idea, you can train it to bring you a variety of objects. Avoid small items that your dog could swallow and make sure that your dog understands exactly what you want it to retrieve. Wire-haired dogs usually respond best to this training; smooth- and long-haireds may need a bit more time.

Dog watches owner for gesture that means "Hush"

"SPEAK" AND "HUSH"

Some Dachshunds have a tendency to bark excessively. Preempt barking problems by training your dog, using food or toy rewards, to "Speak" on command. Once your dog has learned this, teach it to be quiet when you put your finger to your lips and say "Hush." This useful learned routine helps to enforce household peace, and allows watchdog barking to be turned on and off at your discretion.

FOLLOWING A SCENT TRAIL

Dachshund searches for familiar ball by scent

Exercise your Dachshund's exceptional sense of smell by showing it a toy, such as a rubber ball with a distinctive odor. While out of sight, hide the object, then tell your dog "Find the ball." Encourage it to sniff out the prize by using an excited voice as it gets closer to the ball, and a duller voice when it is farther away. Outdoors, drag aniseed in a cloth bag to lay a scent trail, with a toy reward at the end.

PLAYING HIDE-AND-SEEK

A game of hide-and-seek is an enjoyable challenge for your Dachshund and helps to keep its faculties sharp. Begin by hiding while your dog watches, so it can easily find you on command. Progressively, make its search more complicated, but be careful to avoid stairs or other steep climbs. Always reward your dog's successful "find" with lavish praise.

A FAIR EXCHANGE

Dachshunds can be possessive with toys or food. Train your dog from an early age to release any item, initially in exchange for a food reward, then solely on the command "Drop." By rewarding your dog for its compliance, first with treats and later with praise or stroking, you teach it to accept your dominance. Play this simple game regularly to maintain your authority.

Dog willingly surrenders toy to receive reward

FUN WITH MOVING OBJECTS

Dachshunds can develop into energetic soccer players, with an almost terrier-like competitive streak! Dogs like chasing balls because it stimulates their natural hunting instincts. Start by training your dog to roll a ball with its nose; this is a good exercise in concentration. It may then learn to roll the ball to you. Reward with encouraging praise and stroking rather than food treats, which are too distracting.

Dachshund eagerly pushes ball with its nose

THE OWNER ALWAYS WINS

Forget about democracy when playing with your Dachshund. You own all the toys, and you are always the winner. After games, have your dog see you collect all the toys and put them away; this reinforces that you are in charge. Avoid provocative games, such as tug-of-war; your dog might want to win so much that it forgets some of its training. Make sure that play is satisfying by finishing all games on a positive note, with treats, praise, and stroking.

GOOD CONTROL

LIKE ALL DOGS, your Dachshund may at some time present you with behavioral problems. Some Dachshunds are particularly sensitive to unfamiliar situations; others may be provocative or socially dominant. Most difficulties can be overcome through proper care and training, and by establishing positive control.

HAPPILY OCCUPIED ALONE

No dog enjoys being left alone, and this includes your energetic, sociable Dachshund. Always leave and return without a fuss, and exercise and feed your dog before you go out, to encourage rest. Give it a favorite toy or one with a hollow center that you have filled with a little cheese spread or peanut butter.

FRIENDLINESS WITH OTHER DOGS

A well-socialized dog will show interest rather than fear or hostility when meeting other dogs. If your Dachshund's reaction is to worry or become aggressive, arrange to meet a friend with an even-tempered dog. Stay at a distance at which your dog is at ease, and then reward it. Over time, bring the dogs closer together.

Dachshund learns that its calmness will be rewarded

Stranger squats down to be less threatening to Dachshund

Dog sees toy, which will be given as reward

MEETING UNFAMILIAR PEOPLE

Some Dachshunds, especially smooth-haired ones, can be territorial. If your dog is aggressive to strangers, ask a friend to help act out social situations. Find a distance at which your dog remains calm, and reward its good behavior. Gradually train it to accept other people at shorter distances.

Resisting Food Temptations

Prevent begging by never giving your Dachshund food while you are eating, no matter how it may beg for snacks. Offering scraps occasionally to your dog will actually encourage this behavior more than giving tidbits on a regular basis. If your Dachshund begs, command it to lie down, then look away. Some owners prefer to keep their pets in a separate room at mealtimes. Always reward your dog's obedience with approving words or active play, but not food treats.

Accepting Unfamiliar Situations

If your Dachshund is frightened by a new sight or sound, try to reintroduce it to that stimulus when it is far enough away not to be a threat and does not produce an adverse response. Reward calm behavior with treats and reassuring words. Over a period of several weeks, bring the dog closer to the unfamiliar sight until it is no longer afraid. Your Dachshund will also follow your example and see that there is no cause for concern.

Dog remains calm as skater goes past

Chewing Deterrents

Bitter spray, available from pet stores, can control chewing

Dachshunds love to dig and chew, especially when bored. Young dogs in particular can be destructive. When you are away from your dog, give it a chewable toy. To teach it not to chew household articles, spray a potentially attractive object, such as a shoe, with a bitter-tasting but nontoxic aerosol. This form of aversion therapy is usually highly effective.

Dealing with a Willful Dog

Dachshunds are wonderful companions but some, Miniature males in particular, can be willful and disobedient. Be firm, and use psychological rather than physical discipline. If your dog does not respond to your commands, withdraw all rewards – and that includes your affection! Leave your dog on a leash while indoors for controlled handling. If you have not had a lot of experience with dogs, or are concerned about your Dachshund's behavior, contact your vet or local training club to arrange obedience lessons. Remember, most behavioral problems can be overcome when the origin is understood.

FOODS FOR YOUR DOG

DACHSHUNDS LOVE EATING, but some can be fussy. Do not let your dog dictate its menu – it should be you who decides what it eats. Choose from the vast array of commercially produced foods, or prepare well-balanced home-cooked meals. Always keep to regular feeding times.

CANNED FOODS

Moist, meaty canned foods come in a wide range of flavors and textures. Some are high in protein and are mixed with dry dog food to provide added calories and vital carbohydrates; others are nutritionally complete on their own. Canned food will only stay fresh in the bowl for a short time.

Standard variety

Special formula for clinical conditions

"Stew" with gravy

Chunks in jelly

DRY MEAL

Crunchy dry meal is added to canned food to improve the texture, contribute fiber and fat, as well as exercise the jaws.

COMPLETE DRY FOODS

Complete dry foods are a convenient and practical way to feed Dachshunds, especially if you have two or more. By weight, standard brands contain about four times as many calories as canned food. In quantity, a dog needs less dry food than canned food and dog meal. Dry food produces less waste, making it easier to clean up after your dog.

HIGH-ENERGY
Puppies require nutrient-rich, easily digestible foods to sustain growth.

REGULAR
Adult formulas maintain mature dogs on a variety of activity levels.

LOW-CALORIE
Older, overweight, or sedentary dogs need less energy from their food.

TEETH-CLEANING
These large, crunchy chunks promote healthy gums and help control tartar.

SEMIMOIST FOODS

These have three times the calories of canned foods and come in a variety of flavors, including cheese. A high carbohydrate content makes semimoist foods unsuitable for dogs suffering from diabetes. Like dry foods, they can be left out all day so that your dog can eat at its own pace.

SUITABLE BONES

Dachshunds are chewers, and rawhide wrapped in the shape of a bone is an excellent chew, as is a hard, compressed biscuit. Avoid sterilized bones, which can fracture teeth.

Rawhide bone

TREATS AND BISCUITS

It is fun to give your Dachshund snacks, but many are high in calories, and being too generous with them can lead to an obese dog. Use these treats as rewards, and limit the amount given. The more snacks your dog receives, the smaller its main meals should be.

BACON-FLAVORED   SAVORY RINGS   MEATY CHUNKS   LIVER ROUNDS

TABLE FOODS

In general, a diet that is well balanced for us is also nourishing for canines. Never encourage begging by feeding scraps from the table, but prepare a special portion for your dog. White meat with pasta or rice is an excellent meal, but avoid strong spices.

Chicken is easily digested and lower in calories than red meat

When serving, mix rice or pasta with meat to make sure it is all eaten

MEDICAL DIETS

Some pet-food manufacturers produce a large variety of special diets to aid in the treatment of medical conditions ranging from heart disease to obesity. Your vet will recommend the best one for your dog.

Dry prescription food

Moist prescription food

HEALTHY EATING

A NUTRITIOUS DIET and sound eating habits are essential to good health. Provide well-balanced foods in the correct quantities for your dog's needs, along with plenty of fresh drinking water. Prevent begging and obesity by feeding your Dachshund only at set times, and never with extras from your table.

DIETARY NEEDS FOR ALL AGES

GROWING PUPPY
Feed your puppy four equal portions of complete dry or semimoist puppy food daily. Alternatively, provide two meals of any nutritious breakfast cereal and milk, and two portions of canned dog food combined with dry meal. Eliminate one light meal at 12 weeks old and the other at six months.

MATURE ADULT
An adult dog's dietary requirements vary enormously, depending on its activity level, health, metabolism, and temperament. Sedentary, indoor Dachshunds are more likely to gain surplus weight. Feed your dog once or twice daily and restrict the number of treats given.

FEEDING REQUIREMENTS
These figures are only a guide – each dog has its own precise nutritional needs, and different foods vary in calories. Your vet can give you specific advice for your Dachshund.

DAILY ENERGY DEMANDS FOR MINIATURE DACHSHUNDS

AGE	WEIGHT	CALORIES	DRY FOOD	SEMIMOIST	CANNED/MEAL
2 MONTHS	3.75 lb (1.7 kg)	340	3½ oz (102 g)	4 oz (113 g)	6 oz/2 oz (170 g/58 g)
3 MONTHS	6 lb (2.7 kg)	390	4 oz (117 g)	4½ oz (130 g)	7 oz/2½ oz (195 g/66 g)
6 MONTHS	8.5 lb (3.8 kg)	485	5 oz (145 g)	5½ oz (162 g)	8½ oz/3 oz (243 g/82 g)
TYPICAL ADULT	9–13 lb (4–6 kg)	310–400	3–4 oz (93–120 g)	3½–4½ oz (103–133 g)	5½ –7 oz/2–2½ oz (155–200 g/53–68 g)
ACTIVE ADULT	9–13 lb (4–6 kg)	355–450	3½–4½ oz (106–135 g)	4–5 oz (118–150 g)	6–8 oz/2–3 oz (178–225 g/60–77 g)
VERY ACTIVE ADULT	9–13 lb (4–6 kg)	500–635	5–6½ oz (150–190 g)	6–7½ oz (167–211 g)	9–11 oz/3–4 oz (250–318 g/85–108 g)
ELDERLY (10 YEARS+)	9–13 lb (4–6 kg)	255–325	2½–3½ oz (76–97 g)	3–4 oz (85–108 g)	4½–6oz/1½–2 oz (128–163 g/43–55 g)

ELDERLY DACHSHUND

Older, as well as neutered, dogs generally have lower energy demands and should be fed either smaller portions or fewer calorie-rich foods. Protein intake may be reduced to help prevent obesity, which places undue strain on the hind legs and organs such as the kidneys.

FUSSY EATER

Some Dachshunds can be choosy about what they eat. If your dog is refusing healthy, nutritious food, leave the bowl for an hour and then take it away. Repeat this with fresh food at each meal; if your healthy dog's appetite has not returned after several days, consult your vet.

Serve food at room temperature

FEEDING ROUTINES

To reinforce your authority, establish a strict routine for meals. Train your dog to sit and stay, even in the presence of food, then to eat when released from the command. Never offer scraps while you are eating, but occasionally feed a puppy from your hand and stroke it while it eats. This helps to discourage food-guarding.

DAILY ENERGY DEMANDS FOR STANDARD DACHSHUNDS

AGE	WEIGHT	CALORIES	DRY FOOD	SEMIMOIST	CANNED/MEAL
2 MONTHS	9 lb (4 kg)	535	5½ oz (160 g)	6 oz (178 g)	9½ oz/3 oz (268 g/91 g)
3 MONTHS	14 lb (6.3 kg)	770	8 oz (230 g)	9 oz (256 g)	13½ oz/4½ oz (385 g/131 g)
6 MONTHS	20 lb (9 kg)	980	10 oz (293 g)	11½ oz (326 g)	17½ oz/5½ oz (490 g/167 g)
TYPICAL ADULT	22–26 lb (10–12 kg)	595–860	6½–9 oz (188–257 g)	7–10 oz (198–286 g)	10½–15 oz/3½–5 oz (298–430 g/101–146 g)
ACTIVE ADULT	22–26 lb (10–12 kg)	675–975	7–10½ oz (202–292 g)	8–11½ oz (225–325 g)	12–17 oz/4–6 oz (338–488 g/114 166 g)
VERY ACTIVE ADULT	22–26 lb (10–12 kg)	950–1,370	10–14½ oz (284–410 g)	11–16 oz (316–456 g)	16½–24 oz/5½–8 oz (475–685 g/161–233 g)
ELDERLY (10 YEARS+)	22–26 lb (10–12 kg)	485–700	5–7½ oz (145–209 g)	5½–8 oz (162–233 g)	8½–12 oz/3–4 oz (243–350 g/82–119 g)

BASIC BODY CARE

YOUR DACHSHUND NEEDS less routine body care than many other breeds. Its taut skin and finely haired ears make basic grooming relatively easy. Nevertheless, regular attention is required to maintain good health. Check the eyes, ears, teeth, nails, and anal region to help prevent medical problems.

ENSURING CLEAR, HEALTHY EYES

Dampen cotton balls with salt water to avoid loose fibers

Eyes should be bright, clear, and free from redness, with tight-fitting lids. Exploring in rough undergrowth can cause eye irritation. Inspect your dog's eyes daily and, when necessary, cleanse the area around the eyes using damp cotton balls. Bloodshot or cloudy eyes, swollen lids, or a yellow-green discharge may signal an eye infection, which requires a trip to the vet.

PREVENT TOOTH TARTAR

Without weekly cleaning, tartar can collect on the teeth, leading to bad breath, root infection, and gum disease – especially around the molars. Avoid human toothpaste, which froths and will be swallowed. In addition to professional scaling and polishing, rawhide bones help to control tartar buildup. This dog's teeth and gums are in need of veterinary attention.

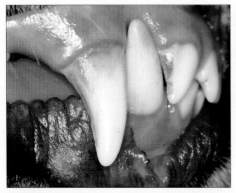

CLEANING THE TEETH

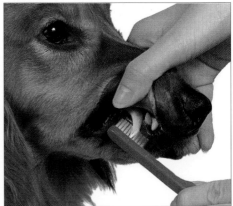

Check daily for any items lodged in your Dachshund's teeth or mouth. From an early age, clean your dog's teeth once a week with canine toothpaste. Using a soft brush, work up and down, massaging the gums. Always reward your Dachshund afterward.

WASHING THE PAWS

After a muddy walk, clean your dog's paws in a bowl filled with cool or tepid water. Use a mild soap that is suitable for human skin, and always rinse and dry the paws thoroughly afterward. Long-haired Dachshunds also need the feathering on their legs and stomach to be cleaned in the same way.

ANAL HYGIENE

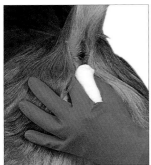

Excessive licking or dragging of the rear can mean that the scent-producing anal sacs are blocked, causing discomfort. Wearing protective gloves, squeeze the sacs empty, applying firm pressure from both sides. Use absorbent material to collect the fluid.

INSPECTING THE EARS

Check regularly for wax that collects in your Dachshund's lopped ears. Remove it with a tissue – try not to push it further in. Look out for inflammation, odor, and material such as grass seeds, as well as food debris on the ear tips.

CUTTING THE NAILS

No dog likes having its nails clipped. Although Standard Dachshunds do not require much attention, Miniatures need more frequent clipping. Tell your dog to sit, and using a guillotine clipper, rather than a "pliers" type, cut the tip off the nail. Avoid the quick, which is invisible in dark nails.

Quick

Nail

Cutting line

WHERE TO CLIP NAILS

The sensitive pink area, known as the quick or the nail bed, contains blood vessels and nerves. Always clip in front of the quick. If in doubt, ask your vet to show you where to cut.

MAINTAINING THE COAT

THE AMOUNT OF TIME you spend grooming your Dachshund will depend on its coat type. Smooth-haired dogs have one of the easiest coats to maintain among all breeds, while wire-haired dogs occasionally need their coats stripped of excess hair. Long-haired Dachshunds need moderate grooming.

ROUTINE GROOMING FOR DACHSHUNDS

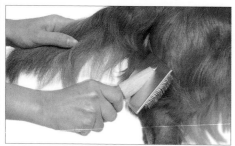

LOOKING AFTER LONG COATS
Use a stiff-bristled or slicker brush and a fine comb daily on your long-haired Dachshund to remove tangles and massage the skin. Afterward, rub the coat down with a dry chamois cloth or a specially made coat rubber to clear loose debris and create shine.

HAND-STRIPPING WIRE COATS
Wire-haired dogs have a fine undercoat covered by longer, coarser guard hairs. When the guard hair becomes thick and is ready to molt, it should be gently pulled out at the roots with your thumb and forefinger. Ask an experienced groomer for help if necessary.

RUBBING DOWN SMOOTH COATS
Your smooth-haired Dachshund's glossy coat is very easy to maintain. Simply rub it down once a week with a clean chamois leather or a rubber pad. At the same time, examine the skin for parasites such as fleas and ticks.

TRIMMING HAIR ON THE TOES
Hair between the toes of long-haired Dachshunds can become tangled and matted. Cut this away gently with a pair of blunt-ended scissors; this helps prevent items such as grass seeds from lodging painfully in your dog's paws.

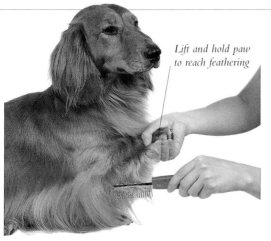

Lift and hold paw to reach feathering

COMBING THE LEGS

The feathering on the legs of long-haired dogs can easily become tangled and should be combed every day. Check your Dachshund's coat after it has been outside, especially if it has been exploring in dense undergrowth. Trim the feathering regularly in a straight line to keep this task more manageable.

GROOMING AS A RITUAL

Grooming is an important means of asserting your authority over your Dachshund. While most dogs enjoy it, some dominant individuals may resent being handled. Avoid problems by introducing grooming routines as soon as you acquire your dog. It should quickly learn to accept your actions as a sign of natural dominance If your dog is strong-willed, command it to lie down and lift its leg, a posture that canines use as a gesture of total submission.

BATHING YOUR DOG

1 Even smooth-haired Dachshunds need an occasional bath to rid their coats of excess oil, offensive odor, or unpleasant material. Put down a nonslip bath mat, then lather your dog well with a mild dog or baby shampoo. Only bathe your dog outside in warm weather.

2 Rinse your dog thoroughly with tepid water. Remember to speak in a firm but reassuring tone throughout bathing. Once you have finished, gently towel-dry your dog, then allow it to shake.

3 Long-haired Dachshunds need their feathering squeezed of excess water. Long- and wire-haired dogs can then be given a final dry with a hair dryer on a low setting. End grooming by praising your patient dog.

BASIC HEALTH

YOUR DACHSHUND DEPENDS on you for its good health. Since it cannot tell you that something is wrong, you must observe how it moves and behaves; any changes in activity or habits may be warning signs of problems. Arrange for annual check-ups, and always consult your vet when you need advice.

ACTIVE AND ALERT?

Monitor your dog's play routines for sudden changes in temperament

Dachshunds are sturdy and vocal house-dogs, and respond instantly to unexpected sights, sounds, and other events. Watch for changes in your dog's usual behavior by monitoring its movement, activities, and moods. If there are any sudden alterations to normal habits, report them to your veterinarian. Remember, Dachshunds are not complainers. If, through age or injury, your dog develops discomfort, it will rarely draw attention to itself but simply alter its ways in an attempt to cope with its pain. Be aware that illness will affect your dog's routines, and that even very minor changes in behavior patterns can be medically significant.

APPETITE AND EATING HABITS

Of all small and medium-sized dog breeds, Dachshunds are among the most voracious eaters. Eating and toilet routines developed in puppyhood are usually maintained throughout life. Even moderate changes to routines can be a sign of ill health. A reduced appetite usually indicates illness, rather than boredom with the offered food. Asking for food but not eating suggests tooth pain, as does sloppy eating.

An increased appetite with no weight gain can indicate a hormone upset. Increased thirst is an important clinical symptom and may be a sign of serious illness.

Increased appetite can indicate too little insulin or too much thyroid hormone

PICKING UP YOUR DOG SAFELY

1 While calmly reassuring your Dachshund, place one hand under its forelimbs and chest, and the other hand around its hind limbs and rump. This allows you firm control over your dog and helps to stop it squirming and paddling as you pick it up.

Dachshunds' short legs make them prone to back and neck troubles

2 Lift the dog by supporting the chest and placing a finger between the forelimbs. Keep the other hand under your dog's rump. This method prevents the dog from jumping out of your grasp and ensures that its back and neck are supported.

Miniature Dachshund receives proper support for its back and neck

REGULAR HEALTH CHECKS

Dachshunds are genetically predestined for long lives, and those that are routinely vaccinated, treated for parasites, and checked by a vet are likely to live even longer. Reaching the late teens is not unusual for this breed. Many old-age problems such as kidney or liver disease can be diagnosed early from blood samples. Arrange for annual preventive checkups with your vet as your dog matures.

Heart and lung sounds are listened to with stethoscope

CARE FOR THE ELDERLY DOG

Most Dachshunds will experience age-related changes because they live so long. Expect your elderly dog to become hard of hearing. With age, its eyes may turn cloudy and near vision will deteriorate. General movement becomes slower. Be patient with your dog's behavior and gentle in your handling. Mental stimulation is the best antidote for aging.

COPING WITH VISITS TO THE VET

From puppyhood, accustom your dog to standing on a table and being examined. Take your Dachshund to the vet before it needs treatment so that it can explore the premises. Ask your vet to give your dog a food treat while it is there, to make the next visit appealing. Repeat trips can be made less of a burden by taking out insurance coverage on your Dachshund's health. This guarantees that treatments will be available for your dog without extra financial worry for you.

COMMON PROBLEMS

DESPITE A HEALTHY ANATOMY, Dachshunds, like all breeds of dog, are susceptible to external and internal parasites, skin irritations, and gastrointestinal disorders. Good hygiene and diet management help to reduce both the incidence and severity of these and other common medical problems.

SKIN PARASITES

External parasites are usually most problematic in hot weather. Regularly check your dog's coat for visible fleas or ticks, as well as mange, caused by mites.

FLEA INFESTATION
Fleas are overwhelmingly the most common canine skin parasite. Use methods recommended by your vet to control fleas and ticks.

EAR MITE
These microscopic pests inhabit the ears and are contracted from contact with other dogs. Keep all bedding clean, and apply ear drops as prescribed.

OBVIOUS SIGNS OF DISCOMFORT

Chronic scratching does not always indicate fleas

SCRATCHING
Dogs may scratch because of parasites, allergies, injuries, or other more complicated internal problems. Sores caused by scratching should be cleansed with disinfectant and referred to your vet. Always investigate the root of your dog's interest in its skin, and seek professional advice on suitable treatment.

Dog obsessively licks hind leg

PERSISTENT LICKING
All dogs groom themselves by licking. However, obsessive licking can lead to hair loss and skin inflammation and may be a sign of an anxiety-related disorder. Licking of the anal region, along with a dull coat or a bloated abdomen, could indicate intestinal worms. As with scratching, your vet can help you to determine the cause of your dog's behavior.

TYPICAL CANINE COMPLAINTS

With any breed, many medical problems can be prevented. Routinely examine your dog's skin, ears, and teeth, and keep vaccinations up to date. Regular worming is essential to protect against common internal parasites, and medication can help prevent debilitating lung and heart worms. Weight control is also important in promoting good health.

TOOTH FRACTURES
Dachshunds have very large teeth and powerful jaws, and enjoy chewing on sticks, bones, and even stones. This can chip or fracture the teeth, often leading to painful root-canal infection. Gnawing on rough objects can also cut the mouth and gums. Discourage your dog from playing with unsafe items by providing suitable toys and chews.

EAR PROBLEMS
Greater humidity inside a Dachshund's lopped ears makes them more prone to infection than erect ears. Check regularly for wax, odor, discharge, or inflammation.

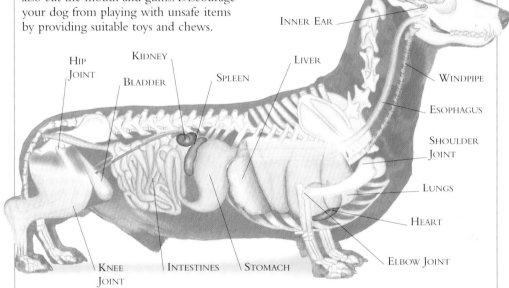

BRAIN

EAR CANAL

INNER EAR

HIP JOINT

KIDNEY

BLADDER

SPLEEN

LIVER

WINDPIPE

ESOPHAGUS

SHOULDER JOINT

LUNGS

HEART

ELBOW JOINT

KNEE JOINT

INTESTINES

STOMACH

GASTROINTESTINAL AND VIRAL DISEASES
The Dachshund's eagerness to taste just about anything can result in gastrointestinal disorders, causing vomiting, diarrhea, or constipation. Prevent serious viral diseases such as parvovirus and distemper by routine vaccination, and ask your vet about effective control of parasitic worms. When outdoors, do not allow your dog to scavenge or to drink potentially contaminated water.

PAINFUL STRAINS AND JOINT PROBLEMS
Your Dachshund's muscles, tendons, joints, and ligaments are designed to support an active dog at optimum weight. Obesity can lead to injuries, as can excessively vigorous exercise in normally sedentary dogs. Over-stressed joints may also become arthritic. A torn knee ligament is a serious injury that is most common in older, overweight dogs. This complex condition requires surgery.

BREED-SPECIFIC PROBLEMS

SELECTIVELY BREEDING DOGS for desirable traits can concentrate potentially harmful genes, but the Dachshund's long history and variety of types mean it has fewer serious inherited disorders than average. However, recent selective breeding has resulted in new problems.

CUSHING'S DISEASE

Cushing's disease occurs when the adrenal gland produces too much cortisone, causing an imbalance of hormones The symptoms are increased thirst, thinning coat, and a pendulous abdomen. The condition can be treated with pills, or by removing the overactive adrenal glands.

Dog's coat becomes thin and loses its gloss

SLIPPED INVERTEBRAL DISK

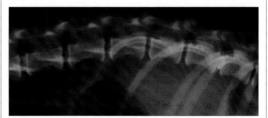

The Dachshund is prone to slipped disks as a result of its short legs and long back. As the X-ray above shows, the disk protrudes into the spinal canal because the membrane separating it from the canal has ruptured. Mild injury causes pain, while severe damage can result in paralysis. The bowels and bladder may be affected, losing their nerve supply and ceasing to work properly.

EYE DISEASE

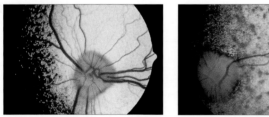

As a breed, the Dachshund is remarkably free of inherited eye disease, although Miniature wire-haired dogs can suffer from persistent pupillary membranes. Miniature long-haired Dachshunds can be prone to early-onset progressive retinal atrophy (PRA), a disease whereby the cells of the retina degenerate, leading to an eventual loss of sight. A healthy retina (*above, left*) is well supplied with blood vessels, whereas an atrophic retina (*above, right*) has far fewer and thinner blood vessels. This inherited disease can be diagnosed in Dachshunds as early as five months of age.

OTHER INHERITED DISORDERS IN DACHSHUNDS

All breeds are, through anatomy or genetic makeup, prone to inherited disorders. None of these conditions is common, and most are restricted to certain lines within the breed. As the study of canine diseases progresses, more inherited diseases are being discovered.

DEAFNESS AND EPILEPSY
Deafness is not uncommon in elderly Dachshunds, and is usually caused by a deterioration of nerve transmission to the brain. Another brain related disorder is epilepsy, which, although rare, can be distressing for the dog and its owner. The condition responds well to anticonvulsants.

UNUNITED ANCONEAL PROCESS
During puppyhood, bones develop at each end, completing their growth at around 6–8 months, when they harden. In some Dachshunds, this hardening does not occur, leading to an ununited anconeal process (tip of the elbow bone), and consequent pain.

SPONDYLITIS DEFORMANS
The Dachshund's long back and short legs make it predisposed to dramatic changes in the back bones. This can result in serious deformity in dogs over 12 years of age.

PROGNATIA
A projecting upper jaw is hereditary in some Dachshunds. This may cause the lower canines to bite into the hard palate behind the upper canines, causing pain.

THYROID GLAND

BRAIN

JAW

INTESTINES

BLADDER

INVERTEBRAL DISKS

STOMACH

BONE MARROW

ELBOW JOINT

DEPRAVED APPETITE
Dachshunds can develop a "depraved appetite," signaled by the eating of feces. This can be caused by an enzyme deficiency; if so, supplement the diet with papaya, pumpkin, or pineapple.

VON WILLEBRAND'S DISEASE
Many breeds, including the Dachshund, carry the potential for an inherited blood-clotting disorder called von Willebrand's disease, or VWD. Breeding stock can be blood-tested to determine whether they are carriers. Fortunately, clinical severity for the disorder declines with age.

FORESEEING DANGER

THE DACHSHUND REMAINS an instinctive earth dog. Outside, it will chase, dig, disappear into deep holes, and even confront other small mammals. Monitor your dog's activities outdoors, and provide a safe home environment. Remember also that cars are the most common cause of canine death.

DACHSHUND SAFETY

Keep your dog on leash to avoid conflict with larger dogs

INSTILLING ROAD SENSE
Always walk your dog on a leash when near traffic, since even the best-trained dog may dart into the road if startled. If a driver swerves to avoid your dog, you may be legally responsible for any damage or injury. Insure yourself for liability and take out dog health insurance.

DEFUSING POTENTIAL AGGRESSION
Train your Dachshund to be obedient, and try to avoid potentially confrontational situations. Smooth-haired Dachshunds tend to be more troublesome than long- or wire-haired ones. If your dog bites another dog or a person, you could face legal proceedings. You may also be liable for property damage caused by your pet.

Steep stairs can strain your Dachshund's long back

PREVENTING BACK INJURIES
Although Dachshunds are able to climb stairs, very steep steps should be avoided to prevent causing injury to the back. The shorter a dog's legs and the longer its back, the greater the stress on the discs between the vertebrae. Excessive strain on the back can lead to painful or even paralyzing disc slippage. Puppies' backbones are particularly vulnerable, and very young dogs should never be allowed to climb any type of staircase.

COMMON POISONS AND CONTAMINANTS

IF INGESTED		ACTION
Slug and snail bait Strychnine rat poison Illegal drugs Aspirin and other painkillers Sedatives and antidepressants	Warfarin rat poison Lead (batteries, etc.) Antifreeze	Examine any packaging to determine its contents. If the poison was swallowed within the last two hours, induce vomiting by giving your dog a "ball" of wet salt or 3 percent hydrogen peroxide by mouth. Consult your vet immediately.
Acid Dishwashing soap Paint remover or thinner Kerosene or gasoline Drain, toilet, or oven cleaner	Chlorine bleach Laundry detergents Wood preservatives Polishes	Do not induce vomiting. Give raw egg white, baking soda, charcoal powder, or olive oil by mouth. Apply a paste of baking soda to any burns in the mouth. Seek urgent medical advice from your veterinarian.
IF IN CONTACT WITH THE COAT		**ACTION**
Paint Tar Petroleum products Motor oil		Do not apply paint remover or concentrated enzymatic detergents. Wearing protective gloves, rub plenty of liquid kerosene or vegetable oil into the coat. Bathe with warm, soapy water or baby shampoo. Rub in flour to help absorb the poison.
Anything other than paint, tar, petroleum products, and motor oil		Wearing protective gloves, flush the affected area for at least five minutes, using plenty of clean, tepid water. Then bathe the contaminated coat thoroughly with warm, soapy water or a mild, nonirritating baby shampoo.

EMERGENCY TREATMENT

With any case of poisoning, look for signs of shock, and give essential first aid as required. Contact your vet or local poison-control center for specific advice, and begin home treatment as quickly as possible, preferably under professional guidance by telephone.

PROTECTING YOUR DOG

Empty containers should not be given as toys

Naturally inquisitive, Dachshunds will chew on almost anything. Keep all household and garden chemicals locked away, and never give your dog an empty container as a toy. Switch off electrical wall appliances when not in use, and spray all visible electrical cords with bitter-tasting aerosol.

PREVENT SCAVENGING

Scavenging is part of natural canine behavior, but it can lead to medical emergencies. Train your dog to "Drop" on command, and prevent it from eating other animals' droppings. Worm regularly according to your vet's advice. Do not feed bones to your Dachshund – soft bones in particular can block a dog's intestines.

EMERGENCY FIRST AID

A HOME FIRST-AID KIT should contain all the items needed for treating common minor injuries. Heart failure and other life-threatening emergencies are rare, but with a grasp of basic principles and techniques, such as artificial respiration and cardiac massage, you could save your Dachshund's life.

FIRST-AID PRINCIPLES AND BASIC EQUIPMENT

The fundamentals of human first aid also apply to dogs. Your objectives are to preserve life, prevent further injury, control damage, minimize pain and distress, promote healing, and get your dog safely to a veterinarian for professional care. Have a fully stocked first-aid kit handy, and use it to treat minor wounds once you are certain that there are no more serious, life-threatening problems to address.

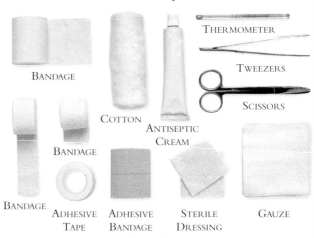

BANDAGE

THERMOMETER

TWEEZERS

SCISSORS

COTTON

ANTISEPTIC CREAM

BANDAGE

BANDAGE

ADHESIVE TAPE

ADHESIVE BANDAGE

STERILE DRESSING

GAUZE

HOW TO ASSESS AN UNCONSCIOUS DOG

Owner looks at dog's gums to check color

Causes of unconsciousness include choking, electrocution, near-drowning, poisoning, blood loss, concussion, shock, fainting, smoke inhalation, diabetes, and heart failure. If you find your dog apparently unconscious, call its name to see if it responds. Pinch it hard between the toes, and check the eyes for blinking. Pull on a limb – does your dog pull back? Put your hand firmly on its chest and feel for a heartbeat. Lift the lip and look at the color of the gums. If they are pink, and when you squeeze the color out it comes back at once, your dog's heart is still beating. If the gums are pale or blue, your Dachshund may require heart massage.

Heart rate may be either weakened or elevated by shock

ARTIFICIAL RESPIRATION AND CARDIAC MASSAGE

Do not attempt to give artificial respiration or heart massage unless your dog is unconscious and may die without your help. If your dog has been pulled from water, suspend it by its hind legs for at least 30 seconds to drain the air passages. If it has been electrocuted, do not touch it until the electricity is turned off. If it has choked, press forcefully over the ribs to dislodge the object. Never put yourself at risk; if possible, share first-aid procedures with someone else or have them telephone the nearest vet and arrange transportation.

Tongue is pulled forward and debris removed

1 Place your dog on its right side, with its head slightly lower than the rest of its body, to send blood to the brain. Clear the airway by straightening the neck, pulling the tongue forward, and sweeping the mouth with two fingers to remove saliva or debris. Clear the nose of mucus. If you cannot hear your dog's heartbeat, begin cardiac massage.

Hold muzzle shut and seal your mouth over dog's nostrils

2 Close the mouth and hold the muzzle with one or both hands. Place your mouth around the nose, blow in until you see the chest expand, then let the lungs deflate. Repeat this procedure 10–20 times per minute, checking the pulse every 10 seconds to make sure the heart is beating.

ALWAYS LOOK FOR SHOCK

Shock is a potentially life-endangering condition that occurs when the body's circulation fails. It can be caused by vomiting, diarrhea, poisons, animal bites, bleeding, and many other illnesses or accidents. Its onset may not be apparent for several hours. The signs include pale or blue gums, rapid breathing, a faint or rapid pulse, cold extremities, and general weakness. Treating shock takes precedence over other injuries, including fractures. Your priorities are to control any bleeding, maintain body heat, and support vital functions. Unless shock is the result of heatstroke, wrap your dog looselyin a warm blanket, elevate its hindquarters, stabilize breathing and the heart if necessary and seek immediate medical advice. If your dog begins to panic, try to prevent it from injuring itself further, and take care not to get bitten.

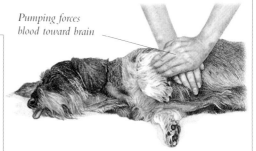

Pumping forces blood toward brain

3 If the heart stops, begin cardiac massage. Place the heel of one hand just behind the elbow, and the other on top. Press down and forward, pumping 80–100 times per minute. Use both hands on Standards and Mediums. On Miniatures, pinch the chest between the thumb and fingers, squeezing together and forward. Vary 20 massages with 10 seconds of respiration until the heart beats, then continue resuscitation until breathing starts.

MINOR INJURY AND ILLNESS

EVERY OWNER SHOULD LEARN how to give their dog medicines and basic first aid in the event of an illness or accident. The most common injuries that Dachshunds experience are to their ears and paws. Since pain and fear can make your dog likely to snap, apply an improvised muzzle for safe handling.

APPLYING AN EMERGENCY EAR BANDAGE

Assistant applies pressure to wound

1 With an assistant helping to steady your dog, apply a clean, nonstick, absorbent pad to the wound. Be aware that your dog may snap at you through pain and fright. Cut a section from a pair of tights and slip it over your hands.

2 While your assistant holds the pad in place, slip the section over your dog's head. This will hold the ear firmly, helping the blood to clot. Make sure that the windpipe does not receive undue pressure.

BANDAGING A WOUNDED PAW

Do not wrap too tightly

Ask an assistant to support your dog from behind. Apply a fresh, absorbent pad to the cut, wrap the pad in place with stretchy gauze, and secure the dressing with an elasticated stretch or adhesive bandage. Your vet can advise on antibiotics or whether your dog may require surgery. Change the bandage daily to reduce the risk of infection.

3 The section will prevent your dog's wounded ear from flapping. If necessary, secure the section at each end with tape to prevent your dog from removing the bandage with its paws. Visit your veterinarian for an examination of the wound.

IMPROVISING A MUZZLE

Muzzle should not cut into skin

1 Always apply a muzzle before you look at an injured area, unless your dog is experiencing breathing problems. With a friend's help, make a loop of soft material and slip it over your dog's nose and jaws.

2 With the loop in place, tighten it gently. Then bring both lengths of material down and cross them under the jaws. Your dog may be anxious or upset, so talk to it in a relaxed, comforting tone as you proceed.

3 Finally, wrap the material around the back of the ears and tie the ends securely in a bow. This holds the muzzle firmly in place and allows you to treat the injured area in safety.

ADMINISTERING MEDICINE

Dog's favorite food is used to conceal pill

GIVING YOUR DOG TABLETS
The best way to give your dog a tablet is in a food treat. If it is not allowed to eat, open its mouth and drop the pill back, hold its jaws shut, then stroke its neck until it swallows.

GIVING LIQUIDS BY SYRINGE
If mixing medicine in food is not practical, use a syringe to squirt it into the mouth, not in the throat where it may enter the windpipe. Hold your dog's jaws shut until it swallows.

REMOVING FOREIGN OBJECTS

Check your dog's body regularly for objects such as grass seeds and thorns, especially between the toes and ears, and, in females, around the vulva. Use a pair of tweezers or your fingers to remove this material before it penetrates the skin so deeply that a vet is required.

BREED ORIGINS

SHORT-LEGGED DOGS have been used for hunting purposes since medieval times. These ancestors of the present-day Dachshund were developed to pursue game into burrows and lairs. By the 18th century, selective breeding from various kinds of dogs had given the Dachshund most of its present-day characteristics.

HISTORY OF THE DACHSHUND

WOODCUT FROM DE FOUILLOUX'S *LA VENERIE*

THE FIRST DACHSHUNDS

In the Middle Ages in Germany, forested terrain made hunting on horseback difficult, and hunters on foot would be accompanied by short-legged dogs that pursued game into burrows. Jacques de Fouilloux's book *La Venerie*, published in 1560, shows these Dachshund-type dogs scent-trailing.

EVOLUTION OF THE BREED

In his book entitled *Natural History*, printed in 1755, the French naturalist Buffon describes a black-and-tan short-coated dog with features similar to those of a Dachshund called *"le basset à jambes droites,"* or the straight-legged basset hound. He also describes dogs with wire coats and a white variety with crooked legs, both of which appear to be forerunners of the Dachshund.

BUFFON'S *"LE BASSET À JAMBES DROITES"*

DEVELOPMENT OF THE DACHSHUND

By the 1800s, the Dachshund breed looked similar to present-day dogs, as this early-19th-century illustration shows, though its legs were still longer than normally seen today. Stock from breeds as diverse as the German Pinscher, Berner Niederlaufhund, Basset Hound, and Dandie Dinmont Terrier had been added in order to refine the breed and give it its modern-day appearance.

EARLY-19TH-CENTURY DACHSHUND

BASSET HOUND
Like its Dachshund relative, the Basset Hound has an elongated body, robust forequarters, and very short legs. It can also fulfill comparable functions in a working role. Basset stock has also contributed to the Dachshund's excellent scenting abilities.

BERNER NIEDERLAUFHUND
The Berner Niederlaufhund, a Swiss dog that traditionally accompanied hunters on foot, has facial features remarkably similar to those of the Dachshund. Short-legged dogs from this breed contributed to Dachshund stock.

DANDIE DINMONT TERRIER
Around 100 years ago, German Dachshund breeders imported this friendly terrier from Britain to improve the wire-haired Dachshund – principally to bring the breed's chest closer to the ground.

GERMAN PINSCHER
The black-and-tan German Pinscher is an obvious relation of the present-day smooth, black-and-tan Dachshund. These alert, versatile dogs have also contributed to the Dachshund's loyal personality and watchdog ability.

RECENT HISTORY

BY THE MIDDLE OF the 19th century, the Dachshund was thriving in Germany and was a favored companion of Queen Victoria in Britain. It was not until the end of the century that the breed arrived in the United States, and Dachshund clubs were set up worldwide. Today, breed standards still vary between countries.

FAMOUS OWNERS AND BREEDERS

EARLY BREEDERS

Although Queen Victoria and her German-born husband, Prince Albert, were the most famous Dachshund owners of the 19th century, the German von Daake family were the most influential breeders. Breed standards were established in 1879, and the Dachshund Club of America was founded in 1895.

QUEEN VICTORIA WITH DACHSHUND

ROYAL FAVORITE

Dachshunds were bred in the Royal Kennels throughout the reign of Queen Victoria. The dogs accompanied the royal hunts at Windsor, and were paraded around Hyde Park by ladies of fashion.

STATUE OF BOY, A ROYAL DACHSHUND

WORLD-CLASS CHAMPION

This photograph of Bergman – a chocolate, smooth-haired, Standard Dachshund – was taken at the international dog show in Hanover in 1879. Bergman was an outstanding performer in the European show ring, and was eventually exported to the United States, where he was involved in setting up the original Dachshund breeding stock in North America. Bergman enjoyed an impressively long career as a show dog, and took first prize at the Chicago dog show in 1891.

BERGMAN

Coat-color Trends

The rare white Dachshund was highly valued in Germany for a short time at the start of the 20th century. The postcard below, which dates from 1910, shows three white puppies, all from the same litter. Today, however, white coats are not permitted by the Dachshund breed standards, except in dappled coats, which should be evenly marked all over. At the same time as white coats became fashionable in Germany, breeding for dapples was also popular; there was a surge in demand for silver-gray dapple Dachshunds, which were bred from chocolates.

WHITE DACHSHUND PUPPIES

Diverging Breed Standards

Interbreeding between coats and sizes continued in many countries until the 1970s, when it was prohibited by many clubs. It is, however, still permissible in countries that do not recognize separate Miniature and Standard sizes. In Continental Europe, the Dachshund is still bred to the conformation standards of the hunting dog, while elsewhere the Dachshund has heavier bones, larger feet, and a fleshier body.

SHOW DOG
Has shorter legs and greater weight than a working dog.

WORKING DOG
Leaner, lighter, with chest higher off the ground.

Popular Images

The Dachshund has been one of the most widely depicted dog breeds in popular culture. This French postcard, dated around 1900, was part of an advertising campaign for chocolate, and shows the buying and selling of Dachshund puppies. The Dachshund continues to appear in popular culture today, especially in children's books, cartoons, and films.

CHOCOLATE ADVERTISEMENT

CHOCOLAT-VINAY

Le marchand de chiens.

THE DACHSHUND IMAGE

FEW DOG BREEDS HAVE BEEN as widely portrayed by artists and cartoonists as the Dachshund. Images of Dachshunds can be found in 19th- and 20th-century paintings and illustrations, while household adornments featuring the Dachshund are popular with antique collectors today.

EXAMPLES OF THE DACHSHUND IN ART

A PICTURE OF OBEDIENCE
Dachshunds have always been a popular subject for artists. This 1912 portrait of a woman with a Dachshund by the artist Gerda Wegener depicts the Dachshund as a dutiful, loyal companion. The illustration was accompanied by a poem that praised the Dachshund's natural obedience and loyalty.

WEGENER'S PORTRAIT OF DACHSHUND WITH OWNER

DACHSHUND WITH BRITISH BULLDOG

NATIONAL SYMBOL OF GERMANY
British suspicions of Germany on the eve of World War I are expressed in this nationalistic postcard. The German Dachshund, balancing poison, symbolizes a nation seen as ready to use any trick during war.

BRONZE CAST
This bronze cast, by French artist Emmanuel Frémiet, is entitled *Pair of Dachshunds: Ravageot and Ravageole,* and dates from 1848. Casts of Dachshunds were popular items in the 19th-century household.

FUTURIST ART

This well-known painting by the Italian painter Giacomo Balla is entitled *Dynamism of a Dog on a Lead* and dates from 1912. Balla was one of the artists who signed the Futurist Manifesto of 1910; Futurist artists wished to represent movement and motion in paintings. Here, the Dachshund's short legs are the focus of Balla's fascinating study of dynamism in art.

GIACOMO BALLA'S *DYNAMISM OF A DOG ON A LEAD*, 1912

FROM HOUSEHOLD ART TO VALUED ANTIQUES

In the 19th century, utilitarian items featuring Dachshunds, such as this teapot of a Dachshund begging, were highly popular. Today, antique collectors have a continued interest in such items.

GLAZED CERAMIC DACHSHUND TEAPOT

A FASHIONABLE BREED

The Dachshund made the cover of the *New Yorker* in 1945, and has continued to be studied by artists and illustrators up to the present day – most recently by David Hockney in his sketches of 1993-94.

COVER OF THE *NEW YORKER*, 1945

REPRODUCTION

DACHSHUNDS TYPICALLY PRODUCE litters of between five and eight puppies, although there can be as many as 10. Before breeding your dog, seek professional guidance to ensure that you act responsibly. Extra care is also required throughout a bitch's pregnancy to meet her changing needs.

THE MATING INSTINCT

Healthy male dogs as young as 10 months old can be used for mating. It is best to take the female to the male's home to mate, since it is here that the male dog is most likely to be able to perform. Female Dachshunds should not be mated until they are about two years old, usually when they are in the third estrous cycle; less mature bitches may not be emotionally prepared to cope with the demands of a litter. A Dachshund's estrous cycle varies a great deal, but ovulation usually occurs 10-12 days after the first signs of bleeding and vulvar swelling.

PREGNANCY DIAGNOSIS

Ovulation, the best time to mate, is assessed by an increased level of the hormone progesterone in the blood. Pregnancy cannot be confirmed by blood or urine tests; an ultrasound scan or a physical examination at three weeks are the most accurate forms of diagnosis.

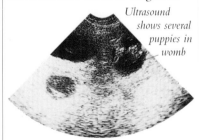

Ultrasound shows several puppies in womb

DEALING WITH MISMATING

Mismating can be avoided by keeping a watchful eye on your bitch when in season. Alternatively, you can use tablets or injections to prevent ovulation, or have your dog neutered. If your Dachshund does mismate, contact your vet for advice. A pregnancy can be terminated by giving a hormone injection, usually within three days of mating. This will induce an immediate repeat season, which in turn requires that the bitch be closely monitored for a further 8–15 days after the first signs of discharge from the vagina.

SPECIAL NEEDS OF AN EXPECTANT BITCH

In the first month of pregnancy, your bitch should exercise as usual. After this, the weight of the litter will make her slower. Walking is good exercise, but avoid strenuous climbing. After the sixth week, food intake should be slowly increased – by the expected delivery date, a bitch will eat 30 per cent more than usual. Provide a balance of calcium and phosphorus in the diet to promote bone growth.

MALE AND FEMALE REPRODUCTIVE SYSTEMS

A bitch comes into season twice yearly, is fertile for three days during each cycle, and will be receptive to mating only during these periods. Males, however, willingly mate all year-round. For the female, ovulation continues throughout life and there is no menopause, although breeding in later years is risky. Pregnancy lasts for about 63 days.

RESPONSIBLE BREEDING

If you plan to breed your Dachshund, seek professional advice from your vet or from an experienced and reputable breeder. Ensure that the prospective parents' physical and emotional attributes will enhance the breed. Both parents should be screened for known inherited diseases or conditions involving the eyes or back. Ask your vet whether your Dachshund should be tested for brucellosis (a canine venereal disease) before mating. Remember that it is your responsibility to raise healthy puppies and to find a good home for each of them.

PREVENTING PREGNANCY

Neutering is the most effective and safest means of preventing pregnancy. The female, because she carries the young, is the usual candidate. Both the ovaries and the uterus are removed, and surgery is followed by a week's rest. The procedure for males is more straightforward: a small incision is made in the scrotum and the testicles are removed.

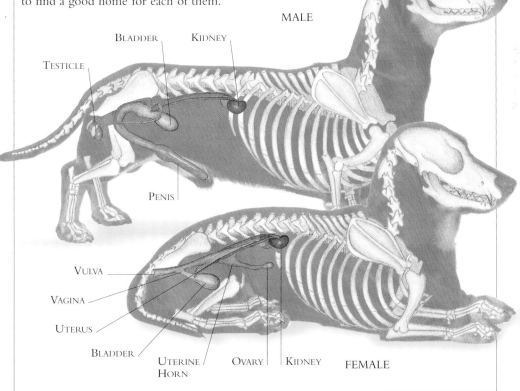

MALE

BLADDER KIDNEY

TESTICLE

PENIS

VULVA

VAGINA

UTERUS

BLADDER

UTERINE HORN   OVARY   KIDNEY   FEMALE

PRE- AND POSTWHELPING

SEVERAL WEEKS BEFORE her puppies are due, introduce the expectant mother to her whelping box and ask your vet to be available in case of problems. Although Dachshunds seldom have birth difficulties, it is best to have experienced help both at the delivery and later, for aftercare of weak puppies.

INTRODUCING A WHELPING BOX

Familiarize the mother-to-be with her whelping box a few weeks before she is expected to deliver. The box should be at least 31 in (80 cm) long and deep, and made of plywood to prevent damage from birth fluids. Three sides should be 10–12 in (25–30 cm) high to stop the puppies from escaping. The fourth side should have a lockable opening to allow the mother to get in and out. You will need newspaper to line the box and to serve as bedding for the puppies for the next two months.

DELIVERY CARE

If you have never been present at a birth, ask an experienced dog breeder to attend, and inform your vet when labor begins. Keep the room temperature at around 77°F (25° C). If after two hours your bitch does not produce a puppy, contact your vet once again for advice. The puppy's position may need manipulating to facilitate delivery. Dachshunds produce long, lean puppies that seldom require delivery by Caesarean section. Put a warm, towel-covered hot-water bottle in a cardboard box, and place each newborn puppy inside. Also use this box if you need to transport mother and puppies to the veterinarian.

SIGNS OF IMMINENT BIRTH

Your bitch may refuse food just before she goes into labor. She will restlessly seek out her whelping box and start to tear up the bedding, preparing a nest for her puppies. Her body temperature will drop from 101° F (38° C) to 97° F (36° C) and she may pant. When her waters break and contractions begin, a membrane balloon appears in the vulva and a puppy is imminent. Keep other animals and strangers away from the bitch while she is in labor.

Expectant mother tears up bedding to prepare nest for her litter

CARE OF THE NEW LITTER

Towel-dry each puppy after it is delivered and clear its nose of mucus; all newborns should squeal and wriggle. During whelping, offer the mother warm milk. Let her rest after labor has ended and all the placentas have been delivered. Place each puppy by a teat to suckle. The bitch will also need plenty of food in the coming weeks to support lactation.

Young puppies suckle greedily

ASSISTING A WEAK OR ABANDONED PUPPY

HELPING TO SUCKLE

On average, about one in seven puppies is born relatively small and weak. Runts are often the least healthy of the litter and, if left to nature, frequently die within a few days. To aid survival, place frail puppies near teats that offer the best supply of milk.

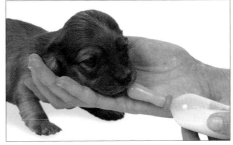

BOTTLE-FEEDING

In large, healthy litters where there is not enough milk to feed all the puppies, or when the mother is incapacitated or abandons her offspring, use canine milk formula. Seek your vet's advice on correct quantities, and initially bottle-feed around every two to three hours.

GROWING UP TOGETHER

After about three weeks, the maturing puppies will begin to explore their new environment; by 12 weeks, their senses are fully developed. Handle and groom all puppies often, so they learn to accept being touched by humans, but do not upset the protective mother. If puppies are gently exposed to other animals, people, sights, and sounds during this vital stage in their development, they are more likely to become well-adjusted, sociable adults.

Puppies still cling to mother for security

SHOWS AND FIELD TRIALS

TAKING PART IN SHOWS and field trials is great fun, but both you and your dog should be fully prepared. Events range from informal local competitions to national championship shows. Your dog will be judged on its looks and personality. Field trials require a high degree of training and obedience from your dog.

MEETING SHOW STANDARDS

Visit shows without your dog to see what happens. To be successful, your dog must measure up to the official breed standard. It should also be happy to be handled by strangers, and have an extroverted and friendly disposition.

IN THE RING

After the judge has completed the physical examination, your dog's movement will be assessed as you walk around the ring. Hesisitancy will be penalized. If it is aggressive it will be asked to leave the ring.

PREPARATION FOR A SHOW

For a show, you will need a collar and leash, a special show lead, a chamois or brush, and a water bowl. Ensure that your Dachshund's ears are free from wax and that its nails have been clipped. Bathe your dog a few days before the show to allow its coat oils to be renewed. Trim the feathering on dogs with long-haired coats, and strip wire-haired coats of any excess hair.

Judge observes dog's looks and behavior

BREED CHAMPIONS

After inspecting all dogs, the judge will often narrow down the competitors to six or seven finalists. These dogs will be examined for a second time. The judge will then award prizes for first, second, and third places. In many countries the additional categories of fourth place (or "reserve") and "very highly commended" are also given.

Ribbons are awarded to winning candidates

WORKING TRIALS

In some countries, Dachshunds still perform a wide variety of working roles, helping both farmers and hunters in the pursuit and retrieval of game. Working trials, sometimes called field trials, are often organized to test Dachshunds' tracking and scenting abilities.

SCENT TRAILING
Dogs have a keen sense of smell, and Dachshunds have one of the most finely developed of any breed. In some countries, breed clubs organize scent-trailing events; a trail of blood or meat is laid along a course and the dogs are expected to follow the trail to its source, using a direct route.

GOING TO GROUND
The Dachshund was first bred to drive out game from underground, so it is no wonder that these dogs show such enthusiasm when presented with an animal burrow. Going-to-ground competitions require the dogs to get through tunnels and pipes. The most successful dogs are alert and leanly built.

WORKING ORIGINS

The original Dachshunds were working dogs. They were used to track wild animals, to bring game back to the hunter, and to drive animals out of their burrows. Field trials are becoming popular in many areas and in Europe, where dogs are thought of primarily as working dogs and secondly as pets. Trials include scent trailing and going to ground. Dachshunds should be trained from an early age for some of these tasks, since they require a high level of skill. Your local dog club may organize such trials and be a good source of training and advice.

COSTS OF SHOWING

Showing your Dachshund does not necessarily have to be costly. If you show your own dog, your only expenses will be entry fees, transportation, and accommodations. However, at the highest levels on the show circuit, professional trainers and handlers are sometimes employed. This can be very expensive, and there are very few dogs that are so successful that their handling costs are earned back in stud fees or puppy sales. If you decide that you are not interested in serious exhibiting, a far more sensible approach to showing your Dachshund is to see it as a pleasurable but minor pastime for both you and your dog.

BREED STANDARD

A BREED STANDARD is a description used by the governing kennel club of each country to describe the ideal Dachshund. Show dogs are judged against this formal index of the unique physical qualities, demeanor, and personality traits that characterize a "perfect" specimen of the Dachshund breed.

DACHSHUND
HOUND GROUP
(Last revised April 1992)

Reproduced by kind permission of
The Dachshund Club of America

GENERAL APPEARANCE Low to ground, long in body and short of leg with robust muscular development, the skin is elastic and pliable without excessive wrinkling. Appearing neither crippled, awkward, nor cramped in his capacity for movement, the Dachshund is well-balanced with bold and confident head carriage and intelligent, alert facial expression. His hunting spirit, good nose, loud tongue and distinctive build make him well-suited for below-ground work and for beating the bush. His keen nose gives him an advantage over most other breeds for trailing.
Note: Inasmuch as the Dachshund is a hunting dog, scars from honorable wounds shall not be considered a fault.

SIZE, PROPORTION, SUBSTANCE Bred and shown in two sizes, standard and miniature, miniatures are not a separate classification, but compete in a division for "11 pounds and under at 12 months of age and older." Weight of the standard size is usually between 16 and 32 pounds.

HEAD Viewed from above or from the side, the head tapers uniformly to the tip of the nose. The eyes are of medium size, almond-shaped and dark-rimmed, with an energetic, pleasant expression; not piercing; very dark in color. The bridge bones over the eyes are strongly prominent. Wall-eyes [wholly or partly colored blue], except in the case of dappled dogs, are a serious fault. The ears are set near the top of the head, not too far forward, of moderate length, rounded, not narrow, pointed, or folded. Their carriage, when animated, is with the forward edge just touching the cheek so that the ears frame the face. The skull is slightly arched, neither too broad nor too narrow, and slopes gradually with little perceptible stop [indentation between the eyes] into the finely-formed, slightly arched muzzle. Black is the preferred color of the nose. Lips are tightly stretched, well covering the lower jaw. Nostrils well open. Jaws opening wide and hinged well back of the eyes, with strongly developed bones and teeth.

TEETH Powerful canine teeth; teeth fit closely together in a scissors bite. An even bite is a minor fault. Any other deviation is a serious fault.

NECK Long, muscular, clean-cut, without dewlap [loose skin], slightly arched in the nape, flowing gracefully into the shoulders.

TRUNK The trunk is long and fully muscled. When viewed in profile, the back lies in the straightest possible line between the withers [highest point of body, behind neck] and the short, very slightly arched loin [between last ribs and hindquarters]. A body that hangs loosely between the shoulders is a serious fault. Abdomen slightly drawn up.

FOREQUARTERS For effective underground work, the front must be strong, deep, long and cleanly muscled.

CHEST The breastbone is strongly prominent in front, so that on either side a depression or dimple appears. When viewed from the front, the thorax appears oval and extends downward to the mid-point of the forearm. The enclosing structure of well-sprung ribs appears full and oval to allow, by its ample capacity, complete development of heart and lungs. The keel [breastbone] merges gradually into the line of the abdomen and extends well beyond the front legs. Viewed in profile, the lowest point of the breast line is covered by the front leg.

SHOULDER BLADES Long, broad, well-laid back, and firmly placed upon the fully developed thorax, closely fitted at the withers, furnished with hard, yet pliable, muscles.

UPPER ARM Ideally the same length as the shoulder blade and at right angles to the latter, strong of bone and hard of muscle, lying close to the ribs, with elbows close to the body, yet capable of free movement.

FOREARM Short; supplied with hard, yet pliable, muscles on the front and outside, with tightly stretched tendons on the back, slightly curved inwards. The joints between the forearms and the feet (wrists) are closer together than the shoulder joints, so that the front does not appear absolutely straight. Knuckling over [wrist doubles over under body weight] is a disqualifying fault.

FEET Front paws are full, tight, compact, with well-arched toes and tough, thick pads. They may be equally inclined a trifle outward. There are five toes, four in use, close together with a pronounced arch and strong, short nails. Front dewclaws [fifth digit on the inside of the leg] may be removed.

HINDQUARTERS Strong and cleanly muscled. The pelvis, the thigh, the second thigh, and the metatarsus are ideally the same length and form a series of right angles. From the rear, the thighs are strong and powerful. The legs turn neither in nor out.

METATARSUS Short and strong, perpendicular to the second thigh bone, when viewed from behind, they are upright and parallel.

FEET – HIND PAWS Smaller than the front paws, with four compactly closed and arched toes with tough, thick pads. The entire foot points straight ahead and is balanced equally on the ball and not merely on the toes. Rear dewclaws should be removed.

CROUP Long, rounded, and full, sinking slightly toward the tail. Set in continuation of the spine, extending without kinks, twists, or pronounced curvature, and not carried too gaily.

GAIT Fluid and smooth. Forelegs reach well forward, without much lift, in unison with the driving action of the hind legs. The correct shoulder assembly and well-fitted elbows allow the long, free stride in front. Viewed from the front, the legs do not move in exact parallel planes, but incline slightly inward to compensate for shortness of leg and width of chest. Hind legs drive on a line with the forelegs, with hocks (metatarsus) turning neither in nor out. The propulsion of the hind leg depends on the dog's ability to carry the hind leg to complete extension. Viewed in profile, the forward reach of the hind leg equals the rear extension. The thrust of correct movement is seen when the rear pads are clearly exposed during rear extension. Feet must travel parallel to the line motion with no tendency to swing out, cross over, or interfere with each other. Short, choppy movement, rolling or high-stepping gait, close or overly wide coming or going are incorrect. The Dachshund must have agility, freedom of movement, and endurance to do the work for which he was developed.

TEMPERAMENT The Dachshund is clever, lively and courageous to the point of rashness, persevering in above- and below-ground work, with all the senses well-developed. Any display of shyness is a serious fault.

SPECIAL CHARACTERISTICS OF THE THREE COAT VARIETIES
The Dachshund is bred with three varieties of coat:
1 **Smooth**
2 **Wirehaired**
3 **Longhaired**
and is shown in two sizes, standard and miniature. All three varieties and both sizes must conform to the characteristics already specified. The following features are applicable for each variety:

SMOOTH DACHSHUND
COAT Short, smooth and shining. Should be neither too long nor too thick. Ears not leathery.

TAIL Gradually tapered to a point; well, but not too richly, haired. Long, sleek bristles on the underside are considered a patch of strong, growing hair, not a fault. A brush tail is a fault, as is also a partly or wholly hairless tail.

HAIR Although base color is immaterial, certain patterns and basic colors predominate. One-colored Dachshunds include red (with or without a shading of interspersed dark hairs or sable) and cream. A small amount of white on the chest is desirable. Nose and nails are black. Two-colored Dachshunds include black, chocolate, wild-boar, gray (blue), and fawn (Isabella), each with tan markings over the eyes, on the sides of the jaw and underlip, on the inner edge of the ear, front, breast, inside and behind the front legs, on the paws and around the anus, and from there to about one-third to one-half of the length of the tail on the underside. Undue

prominence or extreme lightness of tan markings is undesirable. A small amount of white on the chest is acceptable, but not desirable. Nose and nails – in the case of black dogs, black; for chocolate and all other colors, dark brown, but self-colored is acceptable.

DAPPLED DACHSHUNDS The "single" dapple pattern is expressed as lighter-colored areas contrasting with the darker base color, which may be any acceptable color. Neither the light nor the dark color should predominate. Nose and nails are the same as for one- and two-colored Dachshunds. Partial or wholly blue (wall) eyes are as acceptable as dark eyes. A large area of white on the chest of a dapple is permissible. A "double" dapple is one in which varying amounts of white coloring occur over the body in addition to the dapple pattern. Nose and nails: as for one- and two-colored Dachshunds; partial or wholly self-color is permissible. Brindle is pattern (as opposed to a color) in which black or dark stripes occur over the entire body although in some specimens the pattern may be visible only in the tan points.

WIREHAIRED DACHSHUND
COAT With the exception of the jaw, eyebrows, and ears, the whole body is covered with a uniform tight, short, thick, rough, hard, outer coat but with finer, somewhat softer, shorter hairs (undercoat) everywhere distributed between the coarser hairs. The absence of an undercoat is a fault. The distinctive facial furnishings include a beard and eyebrows. On the ears the hair is shorter than on the body, almost smooth. The general arrangement of the hair is such that the wirehaired Dachshund, when viewed from a distance, resembles the smooth. Any sort of soft hair in the outercoat, wherever found on the body, especially on the top of the head, is a fault. The same is true of long, curly, or wavy hair, or hair that sticks out irregularly in all directions.

TAIL Robust, thickly haired, gradually tapering to a point. A flag tail is a fault.

HAIR While the most common colors are wild boar, black and tan, and various shades of red, all colors are admissible. A small amount of white on the chest, although acceptable, is not desirable. Nose and nails same as for the smooth variety.

LONGHAIRED DACHSHUND
COAT The sleek, glistening, often slightly wavy hair is longer under the neck and on the forechest, the underside of the body, the ears, and behind the legs. The coat gives the dog an elegant appearance. Short hair on the ear is not desirable. Too profuse a coat which masks type, equally long hair over the whole body, a curly coat, or a pronounced parting on the back are faults.

TAIL Carried gracefully in prolongation of the spine; the hair attains its greatest length here and forms a veritable flag.

HAIR Same as for the smooth Dachshund. Nose and nails same as for the smooth. The foregoing description is that of the ideal Dachshund. Any deviation from the above described dog must be penalized to the extent of the deviation keeping in mind the importance of the contribution of the various features toward the basic original purpose of the breed.

DISQUALIFICATION Knuckling over of front legs.

INDEX

ACKNOWLEDGMENTS

AUTHOR'S ACKNOWLEDGMENTS

Many thanks to Nic Kynaston, Stefan Morris, Karen O'Brien, Clare Driscoll, and their efficient DK production team, and to Patricia Holden White for convincing several Dachshunds to be positively obedient in Tracy Morgan's photography studio. Further thanks to Drs. Frances Barr and Sheila Crispin at the University of Bristol's Department of Clinical Medicine for clinical X-rays and photos of Dachshund medical problems, Peter Kertesz for photographs of teeth and jaw conditions, Tessa Kerry and Pat Hirst for their experienced advice on breeding and showing, and to Amanda Hawthorne and Dr. Ivan Berger at the Waltham Centre for Pet Nutrition for detailed advice on Dachshund energy requirements. Finally, many thanks to all the members of the Dachshund Club who completed questionnaires on Dachshund behavior.

PUBLISHER'S ACKNOWLEDGMENTS

DK Publishing would like to thank photographer Tracy Morgan for her invaluable contribution to the book. Also special thanks to Tracy's photographic assistants: Sally Bergh-Roose and Stella Smyth-Carpenter. We are also grateful to Patricia Holden White for her advice and help on photographic sessions. Thanks to Jill Fornary, Cressida Joyce, Helen Thompson, and Sarah Wilde. Thanks also to Karin Woodruff for the index. We would also like to thank Pat Hirst of the Dachshund Club of Great Britain, Hors Klebenstein of the German Dachshund Club and Jan Oswald and Jerri Smith of the Dachshund Club of America. Special thanks to Zena Thorn-Andrews for guidance on working Dachshunds. Finally, we would like to thank the following people for lending their dogs and/or for modeling:

Wendy Bartlet; Anna Benjamin; Ben Brandstätter and "Helmut"; Stefanie Carpenter; Roberto Costa; Vera Curruthers and "Merlin"; Clare Driscoll; Jill Fornary; Diane Goslar, "Mocha" (Hyshope Elsa Cream Royale) and "Cammie" (Hyshope Kestral Brown Owl); Anne Hazelby, "Candy" (Evadanne Candice Rose), "Mark" (Frankenwen Top Mark), "Millie" (Evadanne Charlotte Rose), "Reggie" (Evadanne Golden Kuri), and "Teasel" (Evadanne Amba Rose); Elizabeth Heesom and "Frikkie" (Landmark Dark Warrior); Mr. J. Hunt and Mrs. S. Hunt, "Desmond" (Champion & Irish Champion Connnoisseur), "Calvin" (D'Arisca Little Trend at Carpacccio), and "Tatler" (Kireton Cassius at Carpaccio); Gladys Mead and "Teddy" (Champion Minimead Murphy's Gold), "Megan" (Minimead Mystic Meg), "Tommy" (Hobbithill Puffin at Minimead), and "Sheena" (Minimead Ma Griffe); Jahel Kahla; Nic Kynaston; Stefan Morris; Franklyn Morris; Hector Morris; Karen O'Brien; Geoff and Margaret Plaice and the Wunderbarnz wire-haired puppies; Mrs. M. J. Punter and Champion Welcumen Topspin; Sue Seath, "Bramble" (Wunderbarnz Magic Moment at Sunsong), "Corky" (Sunsong Favour Returned), "Dumpling" (Sunsong Serendipity), "Smartie" (Sunsong All In Favour), and "Truffle" (Champion Sunsong Witching Hour); Gina Riley; Jane Russell; Mrs. Lucy Sangster and her Dachshund litter; Stella Smyth-Carpenter; Pamela Sydney and "Jackie" (Yatesbury Jackanory); Zina Thorn-Andrews and her "Drakesleat" working Dachshunds; Sarah Wilde; Dan Williams; Mrs. S. Woods and "Desi".

PHOTOGRAPHIC CREDITS

Every effort has been made to trace the copyright holders, and we apologize in advance for any unintentional omissions. We would be pleased to insert the appropriate acknowledgments in any subsequent edition of this publication.

Key: l=left, r=right, t=top, c=center, a=above, b=below

All photography by Tracy Morgan except:
Advertising Archives: 69br; **Animal Photography/R.T.Willbie:** 9bl,9c; **Dr. Frances Barr:** 56 tr; **Christopher Bradbury:** 70cr; **Bridgeman Art Library/Albright Knox Art Gallery, Buffalo, NY:** 69tr; ©DACS 1997 Jean Loup Charmet: 64cr, 64cl; **Bruce Coleman Ltd.:** 6tl **Dr. Sheila Crispin:** 56 bl, 56 br; **E.T.Archive:** 69cl; **Dr. Peter Kertesz:** 48bl **Mary Evans Picture Library:** 64bl , 66bl, 67br, 68cr, 68cl **Mansell Collection:** 66cl, 66cr; **National Canine Defence League/Barry Plummer:** 24tr; **Reproduced by courtesy of Sothebys: Copyright Sothebys:** 68br; **Andrew Syred/Microscopix:** 54bl **Science Photo Library:** (David Scharf) 54 cl

ILLUSTRATIONS

Andrew Beckett 60–61
Karen Cochrane 49
Samantha Elmhurst: 56-59, 71
Jane Pickering: 39